D1189934

In Camps of Orange

Poetic tales for the deer hunter

Please refer to the inside back cover
for ordering information

In Camps of Orange

Tales of deer hunting from the Pearly Swamp Camp

*Written and Compiled
by Mert Cowley*

Banksiana Publishing Co. / Chetek, WI

All correspondence and inquiries
should be directed to
Banksiana Publishing Company
611 22-3/4 Street
Box 804
Chetek, WI 54728

Manufactured in the United States of America.

Main entry under title: In Camps of Orange.
Summary: A collection of poetry and information directed towards the deer hunter.

Library of Congress Catalog Card Number 93-90585

ISBN 0-9627867-3-X

FIRST EDITION
10 9 8 7 6 5 4

Dedication

To my wife Kathy-

If I was told
"You've one day left
Choose what you'd
Like to do."

I'd spend the daylight
trackin' bucks
That night -
I'd be with you.

Thanks for sharing me with the whitetails.

Your "Jackpine Poet"
Mert

to David -

Best of Luck and Many Happy Hunts.
"The Jackpine Poet"
Mert Cawley

v

Acknowledgments

I wish to thank these people whose assistance and contributions enabled me to write and compile "In Camps of Orange."

<u>Bob Becker</u> - author and outdoor writer from Spooner, WI. for all his research and the use of his articles.

<u>Art Sorenson</u> - my brother-in-law from Ridgeland, WI. His recollections of deer camp provided a basis for many of my tales.

<u>Dick Kaner</u> - WJMC Radio Rice Lake, WI. Dick is deer hunting enthusiasm at its finest. He's the boost that keeps me going.

<u>Bob Traun</u> - outdoor writer and contributor to <u>Deer and Deer Hunting</u>.

<u>Olin Winchester Corporation</u> - the many camp members, deer hunters and their families who opened up their albums and their deer hunting hearts in so many ways.

Foreword

Few men have shown more respect for the whitetail or a greater love of the hunt and all that surrounds it than Mert Cowley.

Mert was one my math and science teachers when I was in Junior High School. It was there that I first felt the deep affection he had for the whitetail and witnessed firsthand how his enthusiasm was passed from father to son to grandson, and to all who were around him.

Years later I was honored to be asked to join his hunting group, and had the privilege of hunting beside him. I savor the experience of those hunts and of the camp life we all enjoyed together, memories which will linger forever.

Life in the Pearly Swamp Camp is no different than in other camps you'll find. It is the work of this Jackpine Poet and the facts and fantasies which have originated from his Burnett County camp that are different.

Beneath the grizzled beard of "The Jackpine Poet" is a man who, on opening morning, has had more than the average hunter's share of success and failure. It is through these experiences and the thoughts shared by this man that one can honestly say, "the impact of Mert's work will last forever with, 'In Camps of Orange.' "

Kirk L. Haugestuen
Principal - Barron Senior High School
Barron, Wisconsin

Preface

I find it difficult to associate orange with deer hunting, for I am from the time when the color was Red. Red, its very mention caused thoughts of deer hunting to race through my mind. Red was the color of my hat, the color of my coat, and the color of my hunting pants. Now they are orange.

Clothes change, colors change, times change, deer hunting does not. Deer hunting remains as it was and as it should be. Deer hunting is timeless, it is ageless, it is deer hunting.

To hunters of that other time, I am one of you. I was one of you then, and I am one of you now. For us, deer hunting will always be remembered as, "In Camps of Red."

To hunters of the present, I am also of your time, so I am one of you. For you, that I may blend into your time, my book is entitled, "In Camps of Orange."

From whatever camp we are in, it is my sincere hope that I have filled a need for many generations and for many generations of deer hunters to come.

—Mert Cowley

Table of Contents

Welcome to Camp -
Deer Season's about to begin

Courtesy: Mueller's Nursery & Fur Shed   Chippewa Falls, WI.

Nehr-Bit Lodge
Burnett Co., WI

A deer camp is often just that, a rustic retreat seldom used for anything other than hunting. Most of a year goes by from the time the front door closes until it opens again.

Ignore the creatures that may scurry when the door swings open, and the musty smells that greet you. Forget the leak in the roof, the front step that needs your attention, and the mess on the floor you just tracked in. Unpack your suitcase, make up your bunk, hang your coat on the hook and your pants on a nail. Your rifles on the rack, and your license is in its holder. Put the groceries on the shelf and big kettle of chili on the stove.

Grab a chair, lean back and start swappin' tales again. Things are the way they should be. We're back in deer camp again.

Deer hunters everywhere would tend to agree, that the finest example of poetry ever written to describe the makin's of a real deer camp is found in the deer hunting classic, "Palace in the Popple."

It is a work of poetic art for which credit to the original poet has been lost in time. We give Olin Winchester Corporation our thanks for keeping it available over the years for all to enjoy.

"The Crex Meadow Camp"
Burnett Co., WI

Palace In The Popple

It's a smoky, raunchy boars' nest
    With an unswept, drafty floor
And Pillowticking curtains
    And knife scars on the door.
The smell of a pine-knot fire
    From a stovepipe that's come loose
Mingles sweetly with the bootgrease
    And Copenhagen snoose.

There are work worn .30-30s
     With battered, steel-shod stocks,
And drying lines of longjohns
     And of steaming, pungent socks.
There's a table for the Bloody Four
     And their game of two-card draw,
And there's deep and dreamless sleeping
     On bunk ticks stuffed with straw.

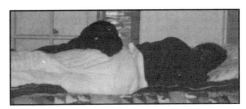

Dan & Honee

Jerry and Jake stand by the stove,
     Their gun-talk loud and hot,
And Bogie has drawn a pair of kings
     And is raking in the pot.
Frank's been drafted again as cook
     And is peeling some spuds for stew
While Bruce wanders by in baggy drawers
     Reciting "Dan McGrew."

Courtesy - Mueller's Nursery & Fur Shed
Chippewa Falls, WI.

No where on earth is fire so warm
    Nor coffee so infernal,
Nor whiskers so stiff, jokes so rich,
    Nor hope blooming so eternal.
A man can live for a solid week
    In the same old underbritches
And walk like a man and spit when he wants
    And scratch himself where he itches

I tell you, boys, there's no place else
        Where I'd rather be, come fall,
Where I eat like a bear and sing like a wolf
        And feel like I'm bull-pine tall.
In that raunchy cabin out in the bush
        In the land of the raven and loon
With a tracking snow lying new to the ground
        At the end of the Rutting Moon.

The Goettl Camp
1948 - 49
Burnett Co., WI
L-R Front: Joe Goettl, "Bucky" Alvin Buchholtz, Bill Weisenberg, Emil Goettl
Back: Gib Hennemen, Mutt Bitney, Herman Dalhlman

They've Earned the title:

"Buck Hunter"

"Buck Hunter"

The hunter of old is admired by many, for it was he who laid the foundation for the present.

He is the hunter of a different time and of a different pace, whose methods we still use, and who is the example we all wish to follow.

The title of "Buck Hunter" does not just belong to these few. These hunters represent the many "Buck Hunters" who have been and the "Buck Hunters" who will be.

Jim Jordan
Danbury, WI.
"The Danbury Buck"

Photo Courtesy of the Fishbowl Tavern
Greg and Liz Johnson - Danbury, WI.

#1 Whitetail of All-time
Shot November 20, 1914

There is nothing new about the story of "The Jordan Buck." It is, and always will be to a deer hunter, one of the greatest misfortunes of all time. Here is a brief summary of the Jim Jordan story:

It was 1914, and Jim Jordan was 22 years old back on that November twentieth morning. Jim was a logger, trapper and woodsman, but above all else he was a deer hunter.

There was fresh tracking snow that morning, so with his 50¢ deer license in his pocket and his 25/20 Winchester cradled in his arms, he took off on what would turn out to be the most memorable hunt Jim Jordan would ever be on.

Jim cut several fresh deer tracks that morning, but one set of tracks was exceptional so he concentrated following that set. The tracks led him down along the Yellow River and headed towards the railroad tracks nearby. It was an approaching train that gave Jim the opportunity of a lifetime. The sound of a train caused an immense buck to raise itself out of its bed into Jim's view.

Jim held a steady aim on the buck's neck with his undersized 25/20, and squeezed off a round. The buck spun and took off, and Jim's next three shots had no effect on the monstrous buck which soon disappeared out of sight.

Jim picked up the tracks and followed them some distance before he found any blood. It was then he discovered he had only one shell left which he quickly slid into the chamber and then continued his tracking. He finally caught a glimpse of the buck, but too far off for a shot. The buck appeared headed for the river, with Jim right on his trail.

The buck, seeing Jim as he closed the distance, jumped into the river, fought the current, then got out on the far bank. Jim took the one chance he had. He aimed for the backbone and fired. The huge buck dropped on the spot. Despite icy water, Jim crossed the river and finally was able to have a close look at his trophy.

Jim was going to field-dress the buck but discovered he had no knife. He left the buck and took off for a knife and some help.

Upon his return, and to his horror, he discovered the buck was gone. The buck evidently had one kick left that had slid it into the river. Jim searched and fortunately when reaching the bend in the river, he spotted the buck, caught up on a large rock.

Jim had already shot a number of bucks in his lifetime, but the drag to move this buck stuck out in his memory. It took a team horse and the help of several friends to get the buck in position to be weighed. Its weight was nearly 400 pounds.

The tale of misfortune now begins. Times were tough and a dollar was alot of money so when a part-time taxidermist from Webster offered to mount it for $5, Jim at first hesitated. But then he thought about how many deer that size might be ever seen again and accepted the offer.

Due to a number of strange twists of fate, that was the last time Jim would see the head of his huge trophy for 50 years.

There is no record of the head until 1964 when a collector of deer horns happened onto the decrepit mount at a yard sale

Robert Ludwig's daughter and the Jordan Buck,
shortly after it was purchased in 1964.
Courtesy - The Fishbowl Tavern
Danbury, WI.

in Sandstone, MN. The collector, Robert Ludwig, gladly paid the $3 they were asking for the head and took it home.

Ludwig knew it was big and rough scored it himself, sending the measurements to Bernie Fashingbauer. Fashingbauer, doubtful as to the accuracy, measured it himself. It scored 206-5/8, a New World's Record.

It was shortly after this that Ludwig took the rack to show James Jordan, a distant relative of Ludwig's.

Jim Jordan could not believe his eyes. It was the buck he had shot back in 1914. It was at this time he had a picture taken of himself and the huge rack.

Courtesy - The Fishbowl Tavern
Danbury, WI

The record head was sold in 1968 to Dr. Charles T. Arnold a deer antler collector from New Hampshire. He now owned the head and the record books, calling the buck "The Sandstone Buck," gave credit to "Hunter Unknown" for the kill.

Jim Jordan wanted the record set straight and did what he could to be given credit for the World's Record.

It was the intense efforts of many including: Dr. Arnold, Peter Haupt of Hayward, WI, the Wisconsin Bear and Buck Club, David Bathke, and Bernard Fashingbauer, to name a few, that finally set the record straight.

The announcement from Boone and Crockett came in December, 1978. James Jordan was now given credit for the World's Record.

It came however, a little late for Jim. James Jordan passed away in October, two months before the announcement.

Jim Jordan died, never knowing the record books would now read, "The Danbury Buck" #1 in the World, shot by James Jordan of Danbury, Burnett County, Wisconsin.

Authors Note:
I had the opportunity to meet Jim Jordan one day back in 1965. My brother had built a deer hunting cabin east of Danbury and we were discussing the cabin when the talk naturally got on the subject of deer hunting.

It was then Jim Jordan told me he had shot the World Record Buck, but I didn't take much stock in what he said.

Now I wish I had.

HUNTER HINT

{ **On days with crunchy cover, walk very slowly and use your grunt call. Make deer think you're a buck, it works.** }

"The Homer Pearson Buck"
Almena, WI.
43 point Non-typical
Shot in 1937

Wisconsin Conservation Bulletin

#3 in the State of Wisconsin
Non-typical
#76 in the World

Story Courtesy of Bob Becker - Spooner, WI.
Written as it appeared in his column Nov. 26, 1992.

Today's story is about a story, one that borders almost on the incredible. Still the tale is true . . . every word of it.

The story spans fifty-five years, back to 1938. Back to when I was an eleven-year-old country kid, half wild, and so imbued with the outdoors that all my spare time was spent probing nooks and crannies of the back country around my farm home.

I'd reached the seventh grade, and my interest in wild things had spilled too into books and magazines; prompting me to make a scrapbook, pages pasted with clippings of timber wolves, moose, fish, and more.

Time passed as I grew older, and I all but abandoned that old scrapbook. But my mother, wiser than I, filed it away. And a couple years ago, she handed it back to me, its pages faded and worn. And in it, this past summer I re-discovered a news story, complete with photograph, of a 43-point buck that was shot during the 1937 deer season in Burnett County.

The story came from an issue of the Wisconsin Conservation Bulletin at the time, a monthly publication of the Wisconsin Conservation Department, the forerunner of the present Department of Natural Resources.

Here's what the old report said:

Mr. and Mrs. Homer Pearson, Burnett County farmers, bagged a 43-point buck during the recent deer season and are believed to have the best "hat rack" that came out of the Wisconsin woods during the season.

Conservation Warden Chauncey Weitz sent a report on the unusual head which declares:

"The Pearsons left home before dawn on the morning of Nov. 28 and drove 28 miles to their former home in the township of Loraine in Polk County. From there they hunted north and east along Sand Creek. Mrs. Pearson had a .22 rifle and she drove the thickets for her husband who was armed with a

30-30 Winchester carbine which he has owned for 22 years. About 1 o'clock Mr. Pearson saw a buck deer with big antlers break cover about 100 yards from him. He fired and the deer, struck in the shoulder, fell to the ground. When the hunters reached the deer, Mrs. Pearson fired a shot into its head to quiet its struggles. After this the deer was dressed and dragged out to the car where it was loaded and taken to the farm home of the hunters, a mile and a half east of Almena.

"Mr. Pearson is a farmer and is very much in favor of the buck law and claims that deer is the only kind of game that he ever hunts."

"The deer was killed just east of Sand Creek in the township of Roosevelt, Burnett County."

"The horn formation on this head is remarkable. The right horn is six and a half inches in circumference at the base, the left six and a fourth inches. The right horn has 25 points and the left has 18. The points are 16 inches apart in front and the widest spread is about 30 inches. The longest points are nine inches long and all points have several smaller points growing out from them."

"The total weight of the buck rough-dressed was 218 pounds which is an indication that the deer is not exceptionally large."

A 43-point buck! And incredible deer!

The more I reminisced about the old story, the more intrigued I became with it. Chauncey Weitz, the warden who wrote the story, now long retired, still lives in Luck. That I knew. Were there others who knew about the deer? Could I get lucky and resurrect that old buck's story, today, in 1992?

My trailing began last summer. Don West, a fishing partner, stopped at the house to visit. Don lives not far from where the deer was taken. And I asked what he knew. "Not much," he said, "but I can tell you someone who saw the deer . . . John Smith. He lives east of Lewis."

And on a recent gray November day I picked up the track again, a trail that's fifty-five years old. I visited with Chauncey Weitz and John Smith.

Weitz will be ninety years old come February. He served as a conservation warden for thirty-three years, most of that in Polk County, retiring in 1965.

"I heard about the deer," Chauncey told me "and I went out to see it. But before I went, I called our Madison office. I thought it would be a wonderful idea to have the head mounted for state exhibits."

"Madison agreed," Weitz continued, "and I was authorized to pay $100." And with that, he proceeded to go to the Pearson home. "But Homer refused my offer, saying that he intended to have the deer mounted and exhibit it himself."

"And that was the last I saw of the deer," Weitz concluded.

My cold-tracking next led me to John Smith.

Retired, he and his wife, LaVonne, live out in the country near Clam Falls in northeastern Polk Country. What could he tell me about the 43-point buck, I asked.

"I saw the deer," John answered. "Homer Pearson brought it into Clam Falls that night. A whole bunch of us were counting the points by flashlight. I was just a senior in high school at the time."

Pearson, later, had the deer mounted. And for some time it'd been on display, Smith thought, in a tavern in Rice Lake.

Were there any relatives of Pearson still in the area, I asked. "Yes," John replied, "his nephew, Ron, lives in Cumberland."

"Great!" I responded. "I'll try to locate him." The old buck's trail was beginning to brighten a bit.

I located Ron Pearson out at the farm he and his wife own near Indian Creek . . . where Ron was born, on land that's been in the Pearson name for three generations, homesteaded by his grandfather around the turn of the century. And my backtracking paid off. Ron knew all about the deer his uncle had shot many years ago.

"It had 43 points that were one inch or more long," he said. "But it had 103 points that were over three-eighths of an inch long."

Incredible, I thought. And what had happened to the deer?

"My uncle had a full body mount made. It wasn't a good mount, but that's the way things were done back in those days," he said. The mount is on display right now in a museum in Marshfield."

And Mr. and Mrs. Pearson?

"She's died," Ron said. "But Homer's still alive, living in Oregon. He's ninety-one year old! He'd be thrilled to know his story will be told once more."

And so, I reached the end of the trail of a fascinating story, one that began for me as a young boy, many miles distant, with a clipping I'd pasted in a scrapbook. And it had ended more than a half century later, practically in my backyard, thanks to help I received from some fine people.

Call it luck! Call it fate! Call it what you will!

. . . I call it incredible.

Author's Note:

As a young man in the 1950's, I recall seeing the full body mount of the Pearson Buck on display at the Buckhorn Tavern in Rice Lake, WI. They had about anything you could think of on display at that time that would catch the interest of a young man's eye. I was a helper on my Dad's beer route and he always had a terrible time getting me out of the place.

One day the deer was gone. I didn't see it again until one evening in the mid 60's when my folks, my wife Kathy, and I met up with Homer in Almena, WI. He was as proud of that buck then as he was the day he shot it. He took us up to his house, opened the garage door, and there stood the buck. What a thrill! What as combination! A record buck and the man who shot it. To think I got to see them together.

Walt Kittleson
Barron, Wisconsin
218 - 4/8 B & C Non-typical
Shot in 1920

#16 in the State of Wisconsin
#179 in the World

*The Kittleson Buck - newly caped and mounted
by Doug Plourde of Somerset, WI*

17

*Kittleson's buck would have held the state record score for 42 years
if it had been registered when shot.*

Walt Kittleson may have been only 17 years old back in 1920, but he already had 3 deer seasons to his credit and a trophy experience few hunters can say they've had at his age. He was only 14 and on his first hunt when he and his uncle brought down a huge buck with 10 points and a spread of 22 inches.

But times have been tough and the bucks are few and far between up around Seeley, WI where his uncle lives, and where Walt chooses to hunt. Maybe this year he'd get lucky and see another buck. In the previous seasons he had tagged along with his uncle and they have hunted for 10 days at a time without even <u>seeing</u> a deer. That never dampened the spirits of Walt Kittleson however, he had the drive to become a "Buck Hunter."

Opening morning, and Walt is out with his uncle and his uncle's neighbor but try as they might they see nothing. By 3 p.m., the other two have given up and headed back to Walt's uncle's house. Walt is now on his own.

Walt is carrying his uncle's gun today for he was lucky to find the firing pin broken on his own gun before he needed it. His uncle had some work that should be done, so he'd loaned young Walt his Winchester Model 94 in a 32 Special.

Walt decides to follow an old tote road around a swamp to see if he can locate any tracks or trails, when suddenly shots ring out from across the swamp.

It is a but a matter of seconds before he hears the distinct sound of antlers, clicking and clattering through the brush. He knows it's a buck, before he even sees it. That was no doubt the reason for the worst case of buck fever that Walt would ever go through.

The buck enters a clearing and stops. All Walt can see is the massive jumble of a rack with thick beams and what seems to be an endless number of branching tines. He knows he must shoot quickly or the buck will escape so he tries to put the bead on its front shoulder. It is of no use, for the gun waves around and he is unable to hold it steady. (He told his grandson Jim, many years later, that he realized the only way he would get a decent shot was to try and steady his aim on a nearby stump first, which is what he did.) As soon as he can hold on the stump, he swings over to the buck and fires. The buck jumps and runs and Walt sends three more shots after it. They proved to be unnecessary however, for the first bullet had connected, and the monster drops.

Walt knew he had a trophy and though money was hard to come by in the 1920's, Walt decided to have the head mounted. The mount was done by Ole Odegaard of Hayward for $12 and it was a mount well done. The original mount hung for nearly 60 years as a reminder to Walt of a day when skill, luck and good fortune all came together, one afternoon near Seeley.

The buck was a highly prized trophy, but it had never had a tape put to it.

It was Walt's son Bard who, upon hearing of the Jordan Buck taken in Wisconsin, decided it was time.

Peter Haupt of Hayward, representative at the time for the Buck and Bear Club of Wisconsin, which in turn were Wisconsin's representatives for Boone and Crockett came to Walt's to measure the buck.

Haupt measured the trophy and when the results were in he told Walt, "If you would have had this buck measured in 1920, you would have held the state record for 42 years. It wasn't until 1962 that they officially measured a buck bigger than yours."

It has been said that Walt's buck, without the side tines, would be 212 typical.

Walt continued to hunt for many years. Most men never even get a chance to bag a 200 pound buck. Walt did. Hunting with a shotgun in Dunn Co. back in 1953 he killed two

200 pounders and wounded another 200 pounder on the same day. The third buck was recovered the following day. Walt dropped his last buck when he was 79 years old.

The evidence of Walt Kittleson's skill as a great hunter and the proof of his good fortunes lie in the fact that Walter not only bagged a record whitetail, but also a mule deer shot in 1969 that was record class. Add to that a black bear which weighed over 500 lbs. and whose skull according to an official "should have been measured, it would no doubt been book," and you have a Wisconsin hunter who should, without a doubt, be remembered.

Walt, you certainly earned the title, "Buck Hunter."

Authors Note: I was fortunate to have known Walt in my younger days growing up in Barron. Unfortunately there were a lot more things on this young buck's mind than talking to Walt about old bucks. Life's old story: I wish I had.

Photos from the album of Walt Kittleson

Big Bucks seemed to come natural to Walt.

Note their mode of transportation.
It appears chains were in order for the day.

A large buck and wolf shot in 1945.

Walt and his son Bard in 1942.

Elof Sjostrom
Seeley, WI.
178-2/8 Boone & Crockett
Shot in 1932

Ranked in 1974 by Boone & Crockett as 10th in Wisconsin, 33rd in the Nation

Photo and Story Courtesy of Bob Becker - Spooner, WI.
Written as it appeared in his column Nov. 26, 1992

23

By Bob Becker - Article written in 1991

Odeal Sjostrom is eighty-three years old now.

Visit with her in the neat white farm home where she lives on the bank of the Namekagon River just outside Seeley in northeastern Sawyer County, where the chickadees and grossbeaks flutter around her birdfeeder; and she'll tell about life long ago here in our north country.

Listen to her, and one will learn about farming stoney fields, of milking cows by kerosene lanterns, cooking meals on woodburning kitchen stoves, and listening with earphones to the WLS Barn Dance show, coming from Chicago, over an old-fashioned battery-powered radio.

Then, Odeal can tell you more. She can tell about deer hunting back in those 1930 times. Odeal's husband, Elof, you see, was an avid deer hunter, who until his death in 1976, looked forward to each season with great anticipation. "His glory was to always get his buck the first day," she said.

And she went on, telling how one year she became ill the night before deer season. "At two o'clock in the morning, Elof had to take me to the hospital in Ashland. Well, I knew how badly he wanted to hunt, so I told him to go home and go hunting. That night he came back to see me, saying that he'd shot a beautiful buck!"

Deer season meant visits from downstate friends and relatives. To "stay with the Swedes" was a special privilege because it meant that Elof would serve as a guide, putting the visitors on stands, then making drives to push deer past them.

"Back then, there weren't many deer. You had to work for them," Odeal remembers. And sometimes, she'd be called upon to help out. "My job was always to help drag the deer," she said.

Hunting from his home, Elof knew the back country well. He'd hunt westerly, toward the Ounce River where he'd worked in logging camps in the 1920's. And there, in the season of 1932, he shot a monstrous buck; the head of which hangs today on the living room wall of the Sjostrom home; a head so spectacular that it ranks high on the list of record trophy whitetail deer taken in Wisconsin and the United States.

"Daddy," as Odeal refers to Elof, "was after him for many years. He was an old swamp buck, living in a big spruce swamp."

"Daddy shot the deer and got his brothers to help drag it out," Odeal said. "And did it smell of spruce! The meat was as tough as shoe leather. If you tried to make soup, you might as well have boiled a piece of wood. We ended up canning it. That took away the taste and the toughness."

"But all Daddy could see was the head and horns," Odeal continued. "Back in those Depression days, he was earning only a dollar a day. The taxidermist's bill was $19, which we were faced with paying a little at a time. But then his sister sent us $20 as a combined Christmas and wedding present, and that paid for the deer!"

"A man from Chicago wanted to buy the mount for $50, but Daddy said he wouldn't take a thousand for it."

Elof Sjostrom's judgement was sound.

For in recent times, a concerted effort has been made to document trophy whitetail bucks. Called Boone and Crockett points, antlers are measured for girth, length and spread. Elof's buck was measured in 1974. It's fifteen-point antlers scored 178-2/8 points, high enough at that time to rank tenth on the Wisconsin record list, and 33rd nationally.

Since then, other trophy heads have been taken and Sjostrom's deer rank has dropped a bit. "But it's still about 60th in the state and probably in the top 100 in the world," said Charlie Weaver, an official of Spooner's Indianhead Rifle and Pistol Club.

When Elof Sjostrom headed out the back door with his prized Remington rifle on that deer season day back in 1932, he didn't realize, I'm sure, that he was about to keep a date with deer hunting destiny. Yet he was a special hunter, dearly dedicated to the sport he loved. And it's only fitting that his name, and the big buck he shot that day, go down in history.

"Elof didn't shoot a deer the last five years he hunted," Odeal recalled. "He still hunted, but he became very choosey. He'd go back to the Ounce River country that he knew so well, and there, often he'd just sit on a stump and reminisce."

I can understand that. Old memories are what deer hunting's made of, you see.

Authors Note: It was Odeal Sjostrom that offered a connection between the Kittleson buck and her husband Elof's buck.

She recalled that Walt and her husband had hunted together many times and that 12 years after Kittleson shot his trophy buck, her husband shot a monster buck himself. Both men had hunted the same Totogatic area that is now covered by Nelson Lake. It is remarkable that two record-class heads would come out of the same hunting camp.

Like the Kittleson buck, Sjostrom's buck hung nearly half a century before it's true importance was realized.

1940
Odeal Sjostrum, Niece Virgina Sjostrom, and son Jerome.

"The Hollow" - 4 miles NW of Seeley, Sawyer Co., WI.

1934/35
Home of the Sjostroms: Rev. Boever; Ed Ploof; Edward Sjostrom; Bill
Vortang; Oscar Pfeifer, Jr.; Thomas Sjostrom; Elof Sjostrom;
and Martin Sjostrom.

Charles Slayton
Chetek, WI.
Ranked 31st in Wisconsin
337th in the World

Charles Slayton was one of the earliest settlers in the Chetek area. Mr. Slayton's residence was about four miles east of Chetek near the Barron/Rusk County line.

Exact details surrounding Mr. Slayton's buck are somewhat sketchy, for meat on the table was of much greater importance than recording a set of horns. It is believed the buck was shot prior to 1900 but the location of the kill is known to be near the county line north of the Hogback Road. The buck was shot with a homemade, four barrel, swivel-barreled, black powder rifle of 30 caliber.

The horns have been handed down through the generations and are now in the possession of Mr. Slayton's great-grandson Gordon Lee.

The rack was a wall hanger until 1987 when Gordon took it to the Whitetail Classic in Eau Claire, Wisconsin to have it measured for Boone and Crockett.

The rack, with an outside spread of 21-6/8 and 19 scoreable points gave it a non-typical score of 207-4/8 which ranks it 31st in the state and 337th in the world.

Julius Stang
Prairie Farm, WI.

Julius Stang and his 160 Boone and Crockett Buck shot in 1937.

Julius Stang, like many of the old buck hunters, was a farmer by trade and a hunter by choice. Each year he would look forward to the deer season, some years getting his chores done early and then driving to his hunting area. Other years he would hunt from a log cabin north of Winter, Wisconsin near Fish Trap Lake.

It was in 1937 that Julius left on Thursday, headed to the Winter area so that he might spend time scouting on Friday, and be ready for the three day season which opened on Saturday.

The deer were not too plentiful in the Winter area in 1937 and the first two days of the season proved to be fruitless. It was Sunday evening when his friend Iver Saxberg and his partner from Viroqua stopped in at the cabin. The two invited Julius to join them to hunt the last day of the season.

Julius took a stand that morning while the other two worked their way through the swampy area below. Julius was standing on an old stump when the rustle of leaves and the sound of horns striking the brush alerted him to the approach of a deer. The deer stopped behind a pine, aware that there was danger nearby. As the deer stepped from behind the pine, Julius spotted horns. One shot from his 38/55 Winchester dropped the buck where it stood. However, according to Julius, the buck was down but not done. The buck attempted to lunge at Julius as he approached. Julius found it necessary to dispatch the buck, only to discover he had forgotten his rope and had to use his belt to drag out his trophy.

He remembers well the looks of envy and the praise he got once the buck was out of the woods. He also remembers running out of gas in his '29 Plymouth on his way to town and being assisted by Warden John Helsing.

Times were tough, but nice bucks were tougher to come by. Julius had his Boone and Crockett buck mounted by Gottlieb Zulliger of Barron for the sum of ten dollars.

The story as it was told to me by Julius Stang, June 1993.

*Julius Stang's hunting shack north of Winter, Wisconsin
near Fish Trap Lake.*

Jalmer Johnson and Julius Stang with his buck.

Hunting Partners:
Jalmer Johnson, Julius Stang, and John Larson.

Tom Bakken
Chetek, WI

Local hunters may be the only ones who will recognize the name Tom Bakken.

Tom never shot the world's record and none of his bucks made Boone and Crockett, but then they didn't have to. Tom's record as a "buck hunter" stands for itself.

Tom is my neighbor, my friend, but above all else, about the finest "Buck Hunter" you could ever hope to meet. In the prime of his hunting days, Tom would have ranked up there with the best of them. Tom was a still hunter and a good one. Over seventy-five bucks would have to agree with that.

Tom's favorite hunting area was to the north and east of Winter, Wisconsin, land of the big buck country. This area was suited to Tom's style of hunting as a solo hunter, one on one, man versus buck.

Written words do not capture Tom's vivid description of his hunts. He tells of how he hunted, one step at a time, never more than three steps, then pause. All the time he was looking, ahead, to the side, and also behind. More than one buck made the mistake of trying to sneak behind him. He waited until everything in question was identified before he would move again. He tells of the shine on a buck's nose that betrayed the buck in its bed, of the tips of the horns he spotted as a buck lie hidden behind a fallen tree. Tom describes with great excitement the huge track he took knowing with almost certainty that it belonged to a buck. It did. The buck was a fifteen pointer that weighed 228 lbs. Tom grins with pride when he tells there was a time when a buck had to carry 8 points or more before he'd shoot it.

I admire Tom, for the hunter he was and the person he is. Tom knew the woods, his rifle, and his quarry.

If my grandson can only pick up some of Tom's woods savvy, then the hunt can continue.

Thanks Tom.

HUNTER HINT

{ Little blood to follow? Have a spray bottle like for window cleaner and fill it with hydrogen peroxide. Spray a mist, any blood present will foam }

Rifles of the Past

No rifle ever made has been more synonymous with deer hunting or has had more of an impact on the sport than Winchester™.

Included below are some of the Winchesters™ carried into the woods by those earlier deer hunters.

There certainly were other rifles, but none have brought down more deer than Winchesters™.

Model 1866

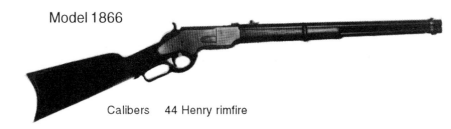

Calibers   44 Henry rimfire

Model 1873

Calibers   44, 38, 44-40, 38-40, 32-20

Model 1876

Calibers   45-75 W.C.F., 50-95 Express, 45-60 W.C.F., 40-60

Model 1886

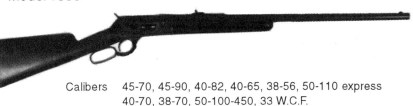

Calibers   45-70, 45-90, 40-82, 40-65, 38-56, 50-110 express
40-70, 38-70, 50-100-450, 33 W.C.F.

Model 1892

Calibers   32-20, 38-40, 44-40, 25-20, .218 Bee.

Model 1894

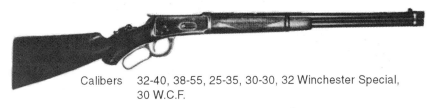

Calibers   32-40, 38-55, 25-35, 30-30, 32 Winchester Special,
30 W.C.F.

Model 64

Calibers available   25-35, 30-30, 32 Winchester Special,
.219 Zipper, 30 W.C.F., 25 W.C.F.

Model 95

Calibers available   30-40 Army, 38-72 W.C.F., 40-72 W.C.F.
405 W.C.F.,   30-03, 30-06, 30-40 Krag.

Model 1905

Calibers available   32, 35.

Model 54

Calibers   270 W.C.F., .30 Gov't. '06, 30-30, 250-3000, 7 M.M.,
7.65 M.M., 9 M.M., 22 Hornet, 220 Swift, 257 Roberts.

Model 70

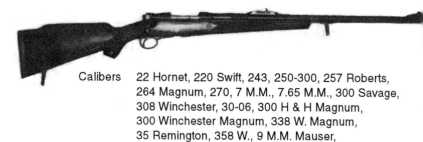

Calibers   22 Hornet, 220 Swift, 243, 250-300, 257 Roberts,
264 Magnum, 270, 7 M.M., 7.65 M.M., 300 Savage,
308 Winchester, 30-06, 300 H & H Magnum,
300 Winchester Magnum, 338 W. Magnum,
35 Remington, 358 W., 9 M.M. Mauser,
375 H & H Magnum, 458 W. Magnum.

Pictures
of the Past

The camera since its beginning, has played a role in nearly every deer camp that has been. It has been the camera that has allowed man to capture memories on paper. It has given man a chance to relive his hunts again.

Pictures of deer hunting are unique, for they are timeless. Years may not be remembered, the camps may be unknown, yet they are the same. The racks on the bucks may differ and the faces may be of hunters you have never seen, and still they are the same.

Pictures of deer hunting, whenever they were taken, wherever they may be, and whoever may be shown, have something in common. They will always show the same pride, the same smiles, the same joy of companionship and the same love of family. Some things never change. For this we are fortunate.

Pictures in this book may show individuals, but they represent all of us. These are pictures of deer hunting. May the picture never change.

"A Face Lost in Time"
Trying to get the grin off his face is a tough thing to do,
when you're standing next to your first buck.

The inscription on the back reads,
"Clearwater Lake and Poplar Lake on the Gunflint Trail Nov. 1930.
Largest buck weighs 267# shot by R.R. Blase."

Photos courtesy of Poor Richards Antiques - Spooner, WI

The hunting camp of Jacob Larson, 4th one from the left.
Hunting camp located at Knapp Stout, Birchwood, WI - Nov. 1923.
Courtesy Poor Richards Antiques - Spooner, WI

Packed up and headin' home
1936

Courtesy of Mueller Nursery and Fur Shed, Chippewa Falls, WI

1925
When the Buck Pole is full
A gang from Chetek, WI

Carl Muerman, Ralph White, Rob Whitmore, Charles Rapley,
Norm White, and Wallace White.

This has to be one of the earliest photographs of a lady hunter.
Turn of the century.

Don't ever complain if you think your camp is a little rough
or the roof leaks a little.

Courtesy of Fishbowl - Greg Johnson
Jct. Highways 35 and 77, Burnett Co., WI

Don't try
← **this** →
these days!

Courtesy Poor Richard Antiques - Spooner, WI

*What better way to bring your buck home than over the
fender of a Chevy?
Burnett and Carl Meurmann - 1942*

*"There's more than
one way to get 'em
back to camp!"*

*There is a better way! Combine a little mink
trapping along with your buck hunting and bring
'em home on a 1934 Ford 5 Window Coupe.
Fred Buric - Backwoodsman
Chetek, WI - 1937*

These photographs are of a time gone by, a time that may never return. These were the days of the trappers and fur hunters, whose skill and accomplishments were the envy of many. These were hardened outdoorsmen, who learned their trade well in order to supplement their incomes, and enjoy the outdoors.

You fellas, you worked hard. You deserve this page.

Fred Buric - Master Trapper
1939

Fred Buric - still trapping
1980's

Carl Muermann
Bobcat
1962

Burnett, Bill and Carl Muermann
Early 1940's

The Beaver Trapper - Fred Muermann

Trappin' Fever

There is a certain time of year
    In the middle of the fall,
When the nights start getting colder
    And the leaves begin to fall.

Then there is a bunch of crazy guys
    That throw steel into a sack,
They fill it to the very top,
    Then throw it on their back.

Now if their boss had told them
    To do this was a must,
They'd throw their arms up in the air
    And quit in sheer disgust.

And then they trudge along the lakes,
    The ponds, the marsh, the streams,
And when they find a certain spot,
    Their eyeball sort of gleams.

They kneel down in that gooey muck
    And set a little trap,
In hopes that they will catch a mink,
    A raccoon or a 'rat.

Then every day at crack of dawn
    They trudge that same old trail.
Sometimes they catch them by the neck
    And sometimes by the tail.

Their feet get wet, their hands will freeze—
    At night they're all pooped out.
Their wife must wake them up at five
    With a swift kick and a shout.

Sometimes they quit their very jobs
    To make that dreadful run,
And afterwards will laugh and shout
    As though it had been fun.

But of course I'm only kidding,
    I'm jealous, you can see,
And if my doctor would allow it . . .
    That crazy trapper could be ME.

The Old Country Poet
Elgie McDonough

There is a fine line that separates truth from fiction, for things happen while hunting that border on the preposterous.

At no other time of the year is so much activity crammed into such a short span of time than during deer season. The intense excitement and anticipation, the disappointments and misfortunes, the camp humor and general nonsense, and the sharing of friends all tend to make things happen.

The following stories are based on fact. These are incidents that have taken place in deer camps around the state. These are stories told to me by folks who were there. Names may have been changed to protect both the innocent and the guilty, but the theme of each story is true.

The Guest©

1991   Mert Cowley

The day had been a long one
    for the men since early morn
Had stalked the swamps and snowy woods
    in search of deer with horn
Quite weary now, with supper done
    they talked and just relaxed
Soon to turn the lights out
    and retire to their racks

Startled by a pounding on
    the rustic cabin door
The men all jumped in unison
    not knowing what's in store
Art, the cook, said "Who on Earth
    would come this time of night."
Then grabbed the old camp lantern
    with the yellow, flickering light.

The light upon the doorstep showed
    two men all dressed in red
Trying to stand, but weaving
    from the spirits that they'd had
With bloodshot eyes and speech that slurred
    they tried to tell their tale
While heading to their deer camp
    they had driven off the trail

"We're sorry that we've troubled you
    we'll warm ourselves awhile
Then leave and make our way to camp
    it's only three more miles"
The gang could tell by looking
    that the two were in no shape
To send them out this time of night
    on such a lengthy traipse.

"Don't think of it, we've room to spare
    you really can't refuse
With spare cot on the backporch
    and a sofa you can use
Just make yourself at home and when
    you turn in for the night
Make sure you stoke the wood stove
    and turn off the lantern light."

Art was up before the dawn
    and stoked the fire hot
He set about preparing
    what he planned to serve the lot
With breakfast made, he counted heads
    to set each man a plate
When suddenly he realized,
    Where was the guest named Jake?

He woke the crew, "There's something wrong,
 it seems we lack a man
Old Jake has turned up missing,
 Let's find him if we can"
They searched through musty closets
 and beneath the kitchen sink
With no results of finding him
 Art said, "Let's stop and think."

"Good Grief, The Porch! he must be there
 I thought we'd made it clear
The cot that he would sleep on
 Should be carried back in here."
With frantic kicks, they jarred the door
 now stuck and frozen tight
And rushed onto the open porch
 to check on Old Jake's plight.

The old man lay in silence
 in a state of deep repose
Covered by a hand-sewn quilt
 and his dirty hunting clothes
It looked as if he'd found this spot
 Laid down, and gone to sleep
Among the frozen temperatures
 and snowflakes piled deep.

The hands of time had not been kind
 to Jake that fateful eve
For any sign, or spark of life
 had up and taken leave
For 'round his nose where once there rose
 his breath of frigid air
Were lined up tiny crystals froze
 to every nasal hair.

When someone pressed against his cheek
    the dent just seemed to stay
"We'll have to check him over
    we can't leave him here this way
Someone get around behind
    and grab ahold his head"
Art said, "I'll look into his eyes
    to see if he is dead."

"I could be wrong, I've been before
    I think he's still alive.
Quick, each man grab ahold the cot
    and take him back inside
We'll set him near the cook stove
    no doubt the warmest one
Then turn him every now and then
    so he won't get overdone."

The gang got Jake positioned
    near the stove and set the clock
To ring each fifteen minutes
    then they'd turn around the cot
For those there in attendance
    it was plain as day to see
That Jake was now the center
    of the camp "rotisserie."

They stood and watched and turned Old Jake
    until two hours passed
Then suddenly they noticed
    he'd begun to move at last
The old man stretched and then sat up
    and said, "I feel great!
I seldom in the morning ever get
    to sleep this late.
This cot you let me sleep on
    it sure makes a comfy bed
I felt just like I passed out
    and slept just like the dead."

Much time has passed, the camp is gone
    the gang has parted ways
But now and then they meet again
    and talk of hunting days
And when they talk of good times
    and begin to reminisce
They all recall a day one fall
    when they helped thaw out, The Guest.

The Boat Ride©

1993   Mert Cowley

Harry and his brother-in-law
    had planned this hunt for weeks
Their method quite uncommon
    for the white tailed buck they'd seek
Their plan was Nine Mile Island
    twas three miles from Durand
The island, closer to them
    not by water but by land.

The men could float the Chippewa
    then row themselves upstream
A total waste of energy
    and time to both it seemed
Twas Harry's own idea, it was
    he who thought and said,
"Let's launch the boat from off this bank
    Look, the island's straight ahead."

They looked and sure enough the distance
    wasn't very great
The boat, the gear, and both the men
    one trip is all it'd take
Bud, he hesitated, and said
    "Harry, this is steep"
But Harry said, "I have a meeting
    with a buck to keep."

Now the bank above the water
     twas 100 foot straight down
Five hundred foot of angle
     not one level foot around
The slope was fairly open
     with some trees found here and there
The ride downhill, should be a snap
     to this avid hunting pair.

They tossed their guns and all their gear
     into the metal boat
"When we hit water, it will plane
     and then we'll be afloat
We'll row across the river
     to the island, and with luck
Row back with loaded cargo
     of at least one 8 point buck."

The boat refused, it wouldn't budge
     it didn't want to slide
"Once we get it moving good
     we'll both jump in and ride"
They pushed and shoved, the ground was dry
     and then they hit some grass
It finally started sliding
     so the two jumped in at last.

At first the boat just slid along
     at a normal rate of speed
"Good idea: for no work or rowing
     do we need"
The boat slid off, the patch of grass
     then hit a patch of snow
Took off just like a rocket
     towards the water far below.

The boat was darting in and out
     and dodging 'tween the trees
Gaining speed, soon both the men
     were crouched down on their knees
"Harry look, the trees are going
     by us in a blur"
The boat continued gaining speed
     to 50 miles per.

The oaks and popples, cedar trees
     and rocks were just a rush
The two were often airborne
     as they flew above the brush
They'd close their eyes and hang on tight
     too late to turn around
Especially when you're gaining speed
     as you skip across the ground.

"Bud, do something, anything
     quick, think of some short prayer"
"Too late for us, friend Harry
     Look, the water's right down there"
It's hard for one to visualize
     but what an awesome scene
A racing boat, out of control
     and hearing two men scream.

And when they hit the water
   one might think the boat would plane
Alas, the plans of mice and men
   are often foiled again
Instead the boat just nosedived
   and then floated on its side
Soaking wet, from head to toe
   this would be their last "Boat Ride."

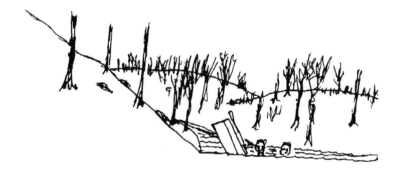

 HUNTER HINT

{ To keep track of the wind, don't forget the old-timers method. Tie a thread on the end of your barrel. It helps remind you the direction of the breeze. }

The Tender©

A Burnett County incident - The Lake 26 CCC Camp

1993   Mert Cowley

They all agreed to rough it
    So they packed their gear and went
To hunt for deer that season
    from a high-walled Army tent
A tent quite large and roomy
    for the men and all their gear
Heated by a wood stove
    while the men were hunting deer

They pitched the tent and split their wood
    Prepared for rain or snow
When done they then decided that
    to town they all should go
They toasted then the season
    Oh, the group had tipped a few
They didn't find their way to camp
    till somewhat after two.

Once in camp they found the coals
    and fires all had died
They couldn't get the fire going
    no matter how they tried
Old Wesley, still in decent shape
    was told to "tend the fire"
The rest crawled in their sleeping bags
    and soon had all retired.

Wes was cold and tired
    and the kindling wood was wet
He shivered as each match was struck
    no fire could he get
At last he had an ember
    he was not to be denied
He opened up the damper
    and the ash door on the side.

He knew it'd take some time before
    the larger logs would burn
It'd take at least a half an hour
    before the damper'd turn
He then climbed in his sleeping bag
    to let the time pass by
And found he couldn't stay awake
    no matter how he tried.

Wes awoke to sounds like nothing
    ever heard before
A cross between a bagpipe
    and a metal banging roar
He rolled himself around inside
    his mummy bag zipped tight
And stared up at the ceiling
    at an eerie orangish light.

He noticed then, this same orange light
    reflecting off the wall
He realized by then that there
    should be no light at all
He rolled a little over
    till he lay there on his side
The sight that greeted Wesley
    caused a fear he couldn't hide.

That tiny stove of metal
      colored now a cherry red
Was roaring like some banshee
      that intended to be fed
The sides of that old wood stove
      were heaving in and out
Groaning like an old man
      with a chronic case of gout.

He knew he had but seconds
      'fore the heat would take its toll
Consuming canvas, men and gear
      and every wooden pole
His sleeping bag ripped open
      as he jumped then to his feet
Just as quick, he then collapsed
      from the intense amount of heat

The cold ground made him conscious
    and he realized right then
He didn't dare to stand up
    or he'd go right down again
He crawled out through the tent flap
    then he lay there in the snow
Knowing that, to save his friends
    back in he'd have to go.

Weak from heat exhaustion
    he lay flat on his back
Watching sparks and fire shoot
    from out the chimney stack
His strength regained, he grabbed the axe
    and headed in again
Crawling on his hands and knees
    to try and save his friends.

He held his breath, and once inside
    the fire still did roar
He used the handle of the axe
    to close the hot ash door
He then reached higher, with the axe
    the damper he did close
And things began, to quiet down
    inside that old wood stove.

He crawled around and shook his friends
    aroused them from their dream
So hot inside, their sleeping bags
    enveloped them in steam
"Get Up! Get Up!" we must get out
    before we have a fire!"
One by one, they each jumped up
    their long johns for attire.

Each man jumped up, to his feet
    and each fell to the deck
It reminded Wesley of the term,
    "A domino effect"
On the ground, they would revive
    get on their hands and knees
And crawl out single file
    to the snow and cool breeze.

Once outside, the men all lay
    in deep snow by the path
Steaming bodies cooling from
    their canvas sauna bath
As each set up, they'd look around
    then laugh with all their might
This group, in soggy long johns
    was a strange, pathetic sight.

That evening before bedtime
    they agreed each take turn
All but Wesley would get up
    to make the fires burn
To go to sleep if Wes was up
    the group had no desire
They stripped their campmate of his job
    as "tender of the fire."

The Float©

1993   Mert Cowley

The doctor Mike would go and see
Would bring it up, "I thing that we
Should go and fish or hunt somewhere
And spend the day without a care."

Mike said, "A river close to here
Next fall we'll go and hunt for deer
I float for bucks in my canoe
I thing that you would like that too."

No more than seconds did elapse
And Doc said, "Great, I think perhaps
That such a trip might do me good
I really, truly, think we should."

Next fall arrived, the two they met
In Mike's canoe they both did get
With camera, guns, and all their gear
To spend the day in search of deer.

They hadn't paddled far at all
Three inches of wet snow did fall
That covered everything in sight
A frosty blanket of pure white.

Perhaps it was new fallen snow
And plus the fact they didn't know
A cable crossed around the bend
That soon their hunting trip would end.

The current moved them rapidly
The cable neither man would see
Twas Doc that hollered, "Hold the stern
If not, the whole canoe will turn."

The cable'd hit him in the chest
And Doc, he tried his very best
To lift the cable high above
But it got tangled with his glove.

Mike felt the lean of the canoe
Twas little more that he could do
So little time to move or think
The cable flipped them in the drink.

Lucky that it wasn't deep
Mike shouted, "Doc, quick try and keep
The camera dry, the thing is new
Doc said, "I'll see what I can do."

The camera saved, Doc raised it high
He said, "I <u>think</u> I kept it dry"
Mike laughed and said, "Doc, that depends
If <u>they</u> put water in the lens."

Mike ran down the loose canoe
And told the Doctor, "See if you
Can build a fire by those trees
We're soaking wet, we're going to freeze."

Doc's fire never lasted long
Although he had it going strong
Wet snow which fell from off a branch
Had snuffed it out, they had one chance.

"We're going to have to paddle fast
Or neither you or I will last
The car's parked down, beyond the ridge
We'll have to make it to the bridge."

Fortunate it wasn't far
They finally made it to the car
Nearly froze, and hands worn raw
Slowly they began to thaw.

Once they warmed and time had passed
About their float the two could laugh
Doc said, "You know, that hunt was grand
But Mike, next time, let's go on land."

The Jeans©

1993   Mert Cowley

When from the hunt Jim did return
There was a lesson soon to learn.
Soaking wet, right to his waist
He shed his hunting pants in haste

He hung his jeans on basement pipe
In hopes they'd drip dry overnight
Jumped in the shower piping hot
The hunting pants were soon forgot.

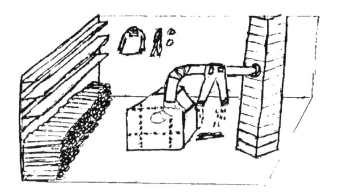

Much later in the living room
The TV on they heard a boom
And then another, several more
Right down below the kitchen floor.

Jim's mom said, "What on earth's that sound?
It's just like someone fired a round"
She'd hardly gotten out the words
When from the basement more were heard.

She told her husband, "You go down,
and find out what has made the sound."
"Why me" he asked, "Why should I go?
You're the one that wants to know."

He had no more remarks to say
On down the stairs he made his way
Then for the light switch he did seek
And finally then he dared to peek.

Timed just right, he watched the pants
Down on the floor, begin to dance
The burning jeans, the source of sound
As the pocket fired another round.

Mike grabbed the red extinguisher
And hollered, "FIRE, all stand clear"
Then sprayed the floor and room about
Until the flaming jeans were out.

He waited till the smoke did clear
His worst suspicions that he feared
Were now confirmed, twas evident
With brass he found, all split and bent.

Jim in haste, as many might
Had hung his pants on furnace pipe
With shells in pockets of his jeans
The pants were blown to smithereens.

A lesson learned, now when he's done
He empties pockets, and his gun
His family says, "Oh no, they're not."
When Jim says, "Ma, these pants are shot."

{ When greatly pursued by
hunters, whitetails drift into
a state of chronic suspicion of
their back track. }

The Lunch Box
Town of Wilson - Dunn County, Wisconsin

Three days into the season
    and the deer they'd seen were few
The group decided they should hunt
    another place they knew
They took the car, and in the trunk
    went contents from the shack
They loaded all their gear and lunch
    in Ed's big Cadillac.

They drove, then took a side road
    where they went for quite a bit
Until it got so narrow
    that the Caddy didn't fit
They stopped beside a sandstone cliff
    that stood straight in the air
Ed parked the car, twas far enough
    They'd hunt for deer from there

Ed opened up the trunk lid
    so the men could grab their gear
The rifles, hats, fluorescent coats
    all seemed to disappear
Everything that is except
    a basket made of tin
Containing all the sandwiches
    They'd share when they came in.

Ed, about to close the trunk
    the lid was coming down
Ben said, "Just leave it open
    in case you're not around.
I plan to put my buck in there
    unless I'm terribly wrong
I feel real lucky,
    so it shouldn't take too long."

Ben on stand about an hour
    heard sticks snap up ahead
He quickly changed from sitting
    he was kneeling now instead
Suddenly a buck appeared
    it ran about half trot
Ready, Ben took careful aim
    and then squeezed off a shot.

His shot, well placed, had found its mark
    no need to fire more
The buck, now on its death run
    down the path the buck still tore
The trail turned, the buck did not
    it now was running dead
It dove right off the cliff edge
    which was lying straight ahead.

Excited, Ben then shouted, "Hey,
    I've got one over here
Let's meet down at the car
    so you can help me load my deer"
He worked his way on down the slope
    then walked the tire track
At the car, he waited there
    beside the Cadillac.

Gathered 'round the car the men
    in silence, stood in awe
For none could quite believe the sight
    they'll swear that day they saw
That big racked buck lay stone dead
    with its feet stuck straight out back
Fully loaded, in the truck
    of Ed's big old Cadillac.

The buck had done a nose dive
    off the cliff and took its fall
Straight down into the open trunk
    complete with guts and all
In case there were some doubters
    that indeed this fall was fact
The picnic box, and sandwiches
    were impaled on its rack.

Ben then broke the silence with
     "It's sure <u>your</u> lucky day."
"You fellas ought to thank me
     That I planned my hunt this way
It would have meant a long drag."
     Ben quipped without a smile
"Without my plan, you would have dragged
     this buck more than a mile."

They tagged the buck and dressed him out
     and then secured the load
They all jumped in and headed for
     a restaurant down the road
The gang, I'm sure, got even
     for I kinda have a hunch
They made Ben buy their dinner
     for messing up their lunch.

HUNTER HINT

{ You can scarcely have too strong a pair of binoculars or use them too thoroughly—though you should not use them until you have first given a careful and extensive sweep of the area with the naked eye }

The One-Shot Gang©

1993   Mert Cowley

Harvey'd got himself lost once
  when he was just a kid
And few men ever had to spend
  a night like Harvey did
Huddled near a pine stump with
  his rifle 'crost his knees
The shadow of a timber wolf
  among the jackpine trees.

That made such an impression
  that it lasted through the years
He loved to hunt, but getting lost
  was always Harvey's fear
A fear so strong within him
  that even as a man
He'd only hunt old logging roads
  and trails where they ran.

Such a trail did exist
  behind the hunting shack
Harvey from his stand could see
  the camp by glancing back
This stand was not a waste of time
  as all his campmates knew
He'd sit all day, and bucks he dropped
  were more than just a few.

Whose brainstorm conjured up the prank
    no name was ever told
But it centered 'round a head mount
    that was several decades old
An auction had produced the head
    two dollars paid in all
It started wheels turning
    how they'd use it in the fall.

Fall arrived, tomorrow was
    the opener no doubt
Unpacked, old Harvey walked right down
    to check his deer stand out
"The sign is good" as he returned
    "there's rubs and lots of tracks
With any luck, I'll drop my buck
    right here, behind the shack."

Harvey stretched out on his bunk
    some rest he hoped to get
This gave his campmates time enough
    to get the prank all set
Silently from Roy's old truck
    the headmount in their hand
They hiked down Harvey's trail
    Several yards beyond his stand.

Twas there among some buckbrush
    that they hung the full head mount
Wired to a popple tree
    its nose and horns peered out
It looked just like a real buck
    staring up the trail
That in the light, of early morn
    they knew it wouldn't fail.

Next morning bright and early
      after all the men were fed
They sat and drank their coffee
      then to their stands they'd head
Twas Roy who broke the silence with
      this comment short and blunt
"You know this year, we all should add
      excitement to our hunt."

"We all have gotten several bucks
      there's none of us who've not
And shooting at the rifle range
      We know we're all crack shots
Right here and now, I do suggest
      our hunting thrills renew
Let's call ourselves "The One-Shot Gang"
      may all our shots be true."

All but Harvey knew that this
      was just part of a plan
So Roy called for a vote right then,
      and each man raised his hand
At first he was reluctant
      but then he joined the rest
He'd see quite soon, if with one shell
      he too could pass the test.

His campmates stood, they emptied out
      their pockets and their clips
On the table laying shells
      with lead and copper tips
Harvey, he was last in line
      but finally he agreed
"Who needs a pocket full of shells?
      One bullet's all I'll need."

From each pile, Roy then took
    a bullet for each man
Then one by one they'd file by
    he'd place it in their hand
It was a ceremony
    and when over Roy did tell
"Members of the 'The One-Shot Gang'
    Go forth, and use it well."

Harvey said "I'm gonna leave
    and head down to my stand
I like to watch as daybreak comes
    and lights the forest land"
Outside he loaded up his gun
    and eased the hammer down
Then took the trail towards his stand
    and walked without a sound.

It was that time of morning
    neither dark nor really light
Harvey'd walked up on a doe
    and startled it to flight
Quietly he reached his stand
    his stump that seldom failed
Twas then he saw the object,
    Standing there beside the trail.

Harvey strained his eyes until
    they both began to tear
No matter how he tried he couldn't
    make it out too clear
Woodswise as old Harvey was
    he didn't dare to move
For if that was, a buck up there
    this chance he'd surely lose.

It felt like time was frozen
    till it'd finally gotten light
Enough so Harvey dared to use
    his telescopic sight
His scope picked up what light there was
    enough so he could see
He then made out, a trophy buck
    big as big could be.

The outside spread on that old buck
    was twenty-three or four
It's neck so swollen that in rut
    it'd been a month or more
Harvey started shaking
    and his forehead bead with sweat
A nicer shot at such a buck
    he knew he'd never get.

With his thumb he slowly moved
    the hammer back to cock
He took a breath, and eased it out
    his cheek against the stock
He slowly moved the crosshairs
    as he rested 'gainst a tree
Then slowly squeezed the trigger
    aiming where the chest should be.

The rifle cracked, from what he saw
    that old buck never flinched
He knew his gun was zeroed in
    to shoot within an inch
He quickly levered in a round, then aimed
    the gun went "click."
It dawned on him, "I've shot my shell"
    the thought just made him sick.

Some say that was the only chance
    that Harvey ever had
To bag a trophy whitetail buck
    he wanted real bad
His shot had been, a total miss
    no time to wonder why
That big old buck still stood there,
    they were staring eye to eye.

Afraid that he might scare the buck
    and make it run away
Slowly he backed up the trail
    nearly all the way
Sensing he was near the shack
    he spun and made a dash
Leaping several feet and steps
    and through the door he crashed.

"We heard you shoot" his campmates said
    "Tell us, what'd you get?"
"No time to talk! I need some shells!
    I haven't got him yet!
Just hand me some, I need them bad
    another four or five
I know I had to hit that buck
    but the darned thing's still alive!"

Solemn faced, twas Roy who spoke
    "You want more shells right now?
It hasn't been ten minutes
    since you stood and took a vow.
Harvey, you should know by now
    to stand and say an oath
You don't just choose the parts you like
    and take the best of both."

At first he was demanding, Harvey said
    "No chance is greater!
I want a handfull right away
    we'll talk about it later!"
Roy, just stood and held his ground
    when he saw this didn't work.
Old Harvey said, "I mean Right <u>NOW</u>
    or someone will get hurt!"

He turned then to his campmates
    as he searched for some support
When no one offered any help
    he had one last resort
Harvey dropped down on his knees
    and started then to beg
Tears were welling in his eyes
    as he clung to Roy's left leg.

"Please, oh Please, I beg of you
    I only need one shell
That buck's so big, it has to be
    a fugitive from Hell!
I know it's wrong to ask you"
    as he tugged on Roy's wool pants
"I know this is, 'The One-Shot Gang,'
    but I need another chance."

Harvey'd been so busy
  while he'd begged for three or four
He never saw two campmates sneak
  behind him out the door
Then scamper down the trail
  just as quickly as could be
They then removed that mounted head
  from off the popple tree.

Roy appeared to weaken
  like he'd finally given in
"Harvey, here's another shell
  go after him again."
"Thank you Roy, I owe you"
  as he took off on the run.
Harvey racing to his stand
  as he loaded up his gun.

Sprinting down the trail
  so it didn't take too long
Ready to take careful aim
  but the monster buck was gone
They swear that Harvey's voice was heard
  for miles, these words rang
"I wish to Hell, I'd never joined
  'The Jackpine One-Shot Gang.' "

The Coloring©

1993   Mert Cowley

It happened just like clockwork
    the same thing every year
The night before the opener
    this camp mate would appear
Standing in the doorway
    uninvited as could be
He'd eat, and sleep, and share the fun
    and do it all for free.

No knock, the door would open
    he'd announce, "Well here I am,
I hope you're serving something
    'sides the same hot dish again"
He'd toss his bedroll on a bunk
    then say, "the quilts are damp
You guys should take much better care,
    of this old hunting camp."

Now it wasn't that the gang disliked
    this man for who he was
For once in camp, he'd do his share
    like any member does
At cards he'd raise the ante up
    then donate to the pot
The money he lost playing cards
    helped cover costs alot.

But Lyell, leader of the camp
    declared, "Enough's enough!
Next year when Clarence shows up
    I'm going to call his bluff
I have my plans all ready
    for next year you guys will see
Clarence, he will entertain
    and do it all for free."

Sure enough, next season
    like it'd been for years and years
Clarence, uninvited, came to
    hunt the whitetail deer
And Lyell'd told the others
    "Now what happens, just ignore
Clarence, he will pay a price
    like he's never paid before."

All settled in and supper done
    the dishes washed and dry
Clarence said, "It's poker time
    if any dare to try"
He took the deck and slammed it
    on the table with a thud
"Lyell, you can cut them
    the game is five card stud."

The game of cards went smoothly
    and each man'd dealt his turn
Then Lyell stood, between two hands
    and said "I shall return"
He walked then over to the case
    kept cold there on the floor
He said, "I need another one,
    do you guys need some more?"

Then Clarence spoke "Yeh Lyell,
    grab another brew for me
That salty tasting meatloaf
    made me thirsty as could be"
Those words were just exactly what
    Lyell'd hoped to hear
He never hesitated as
    he grabbed another beer.

His back to Clarence he removed
    the cap from off the top
Then from a tiny bottle poured
    its contents, every drop
The bottle had held food dye
    the coloring was blue
He turned and said to Clarence
    "Here, this one's just for you."

Clarence smacked his lips before
      he even took a drink
And said, "I'll tell you fellas
      just exactly what I think"
He took two swigs, and then declared,
      "If I ever had a guess
Good times, good friends, they just don't make
      it any better than this."

A few hands later Clarence said,
      "just deal me right in.
I'll need about a minute
      then I'm coming right back in."
He stepped out to relieve himself
      it didn't take too long
The porch light on the snowbank
      showed him something really wrong.

They heard his footsteps pounding
      as he raced acrossed the porch
Screaming like a tomcat
      that'd had its tail scorched
He swung the front door open
      and with terror in his eye
Said, "take me to a doctor,
      I think I'm going to die."

Nonchalant the gang then looked
      at Clarence standing there
And said, "Are you still playing?
      You've got to beat a pair."
Frantic, Clarence raced around
      and finally found a mirror
As he looked at his reflection
      he stared in utter fear.

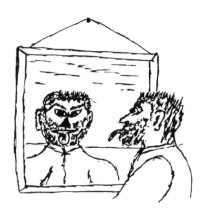

He quickly stuck his tongue out
    and discovered it was blue
His lips, the whites of both his eyes
    had taken on that hue
Even skin around his cheeks
    was colored, yet was pale
The cuticles bore shades of blue
    beneath his fingernails.

"Someone help me" Clarence begged
    "I haven't got too long"
The gang, they just kept playing cards
    like not a thing was wrong
One spoke then as they shuffled and said,
    "Sleep should make things right
You'll be all right by morning
    if you make it through the night."

Sure enough by morning
    all the coloring was gone
The gang they all told Clarence
    there was really nothing wrong
"We've diagnosed your problem,
    and Lyell said he bet
That coloring, it might be traced
    to what you drank, or what you et."

Deer Hunting

A Family
Affair

The Mert Cowley Crew

*Mert Cowley, Sr.
Buck taken east of Danbury,
Burnett Co., WI - 1966*

*Burnett Co., WI
1992*

*Dan hunts so far off the
beaten path, Dave calls
his stand Cambodia—
but look who's
helping who.*

*Here's a pair to draw to!
Dan & Mert Cowley
1992*

*The present and the future of the Cowley
Crew.*

*Mert's Blackpowder Bear.
Taken with a 45 cal. TC Seneca.
October 3, 1993*

The Pearly Swamp Camp
1992

Dave & Dan - ready to head out.

*Mert's Blackpowder Buck.
Taken with a 45 cal. TC Seneca.
The only deer seen in 7 days of hunting.*

*Dan's Buck - 8 pt. 18" spread.
Opening morning.*

Rick Hill's First Buck - Sunday.

*Dave and Dan do the work with
Bill Rhiger giving directions.*

The Pearly Swamp Activities

We pray for tracking snow every night at the Pearly Swamp Camp.

Beans, a few onions, and a venison steak sandwich fixed in the woods makes a mean lunch. We haven't lost a man to starvation yet.

Dan is not only a good buck hunter, he handles a fork real well also.

1991 Blackpowder Buck. Some of us use the snow to track deer.

Bill uses the snow to make tracks.

The Pearly Swamp Activities

Dan and Mert Cowley
Two bucks on the "The Buck Hauler."
It's a '29 Ford Model A on a 4-wheel drive '66 Scout Chassis.
Crude but it does the job.
1981

Louie and Buefort
A Hunt to Remember

You always called him "Louie"
    though you two had never met
"Big Louie" was the big buck
    That it never seemed you'd get
Then from a swamp, he came this year
    to cross his path with you
Your dream became reality
    in nineteen ninety-two.

I wasn't there to help you
    not beside you anyway
to offer my assistance
    when you took his track that day
But stories that I'd told you
    of what bucks so often do
Helped keep you on his trail
    when he tried to backtrack you.

I'd had the chance, so many times
  to bag a trophy deer
They all escaped for reasons
  that to me were never clear
This year things came together
  with the help I got from you
I finally bagged "Old Buefort"
  in nineteen ninety-two.

And you weren't there beside me
  when that buck came past my stand
But it was you who pushed him
  from that slashed off popple land
And if you hadn't gone ahead
  when I took Buefort's trail
There would have been, a different end
  to this happy hunting tale.

Bucks like this, we may not find
  for many years again
These words must be remembered
  long before the season's end
"Should luck seem hard to come by
  or the bucks you hunt are few
Think back in time, to hunts we shared
  in nineteen ninety-two."

To Dan from Dad 1992

The Mike Cowley Crew
Barron, WI

*Mike Cowley - Buffalo Co., WI 1991
Hunger Gang - Fountain City, WI.*

*Mike and Missy Cowley
Polk Co. Buck - 1975*

*Careful planning makes for a good set of drivers
Buffalo Co. - 1991
Mike, Tom, Collin, Tony, and Jim Cowley.*

*Tom Cowley - 1st Buck
Barron Co., WI*

The Buchholtz's
New Auburn, WI

Alvin Buchholtz's Buck
Site of the Goettl Camp
Burnett County - Danbury, WI.

Bill Buchholtz - 1981
Chippewa Co., WI

Josh Buchholtz
1st Buck - Chippewa Co., WI
1988

Jamie Buchholtz
1st Buck - Chippewa Co., WI.
1992

The Gordon Lee Gang
Chetek, WI

Slayton Gang - 1920's
1st - W.C. Slayton; 7th - Albert Slayton

Gordon Lee, Sr.
1958 - 11 pt. Buck
Shot north of Ladysmith
Sawyer Co., WI

Gordon Lee
1989
10 pt. Blue Hills Buck
Rusk Co., WI

Jon Lee
1986
9 pointer
Barron Co., WI

Tom Lee
1985
10 pointer
Barron Co., WI

Andy Lee
1988
9 pt. Blue Hills Buck
Rusk Co., WI

Miriam Lee
1979
11" Spiker
Barron Co., WI

The Lee Gang Cont'd

Sarah Lee
7 pt. Blue Hills Buck
Rusk Co., WI

Richard Huset
1961 - 1st Hunt, 1st Buck
12 yrs. old with 38/40 Winchester
Sawyer Co., WI

Buck Pole at the Lee Camp - Blue Hills,
Rusk Co., WI
Andy, Tom, Gordon, Kevin Turany, Jon.

Tom Lee and the "Pinto Buck."

5 Generations of Deer Hunting Success
These Bucks were taken by Gordon Jr.'s:
Great Grandfather - Charles Slayton
Grandfather - C.W. Slayton
Father - Gordon Sr.
Son - Tom's "Pinto" Buck
and two of Gordon's own bucks.

The Kamrath Gang
Cameron, WI

Otto Lucht & Chuck Kamrath

Herman Raawe's Buck - 1951

*Bruce Kamrath, Chuck Kamrath
Barry Kamrath*

1971

Chuck Kamrath	*Al Raawe*
Bruce Kamrath	*Jeff Kamrath*
Kevin Kamrath	*Ken Kamrath*

Chuck Kamrath - 1969

The Kamrath Gang Cont'd

Bruce Kamrath
and son Christopher - 1991

Dale Kamrath
"May his hunts always continue."

Chuck Kamrath - 1991

Ken Kamrath - 1959

John Wiener - 10 pt., 200 pounds
1991

Terry Wirner - 7 pt.

Camp Foolishness
(Come to think of it that's a dandy
name for any deer camp.)

Deer hunting, as we all know by now, is serious business. One must always stay wide awake and on his toes, for who knows when that big buck might come crashing out of the swamp.

Come to think of it, one can only be legally in the woods 10 hours out of a day. That leaves 14 hours out of a day to relax and prepare for tomorrows hunt. After all, who in their right mind would expect you to stay at full alert all day long?

Witness if you will, hunters during these hours as they attempt to improve not only the skills required of them as hunters, but also improve themselves, in order that they may become better campmates.

In order to be a good campmate, you
must learn to share. In camp the motto
is, "All for one, and one for all."

A good hunter must learn to concentrate.
Try and think, "If I were a buck, where
would I be right now?"

To improve yourself as a hunter,
learn all you can about your quarry.
Read - Read - Read.

If deer are avoiding you, try a
disguise. Look at it this way, if you
can't fight em why not join 'em?

Condition yourself so you are
prepared for any obstacles you
might encounter while on the trail.

Above all, learn to be very quiet
and don't move while on stand.
Patience pays off.

There appears to be a question here of who fired the fatal shot. Think before you reach this point. "sticks and stones may break my bones."

There's one in every camp. He's the guy that's always bragging he could "bring 'em back alive." May the horns of a thousand bucks gore your butt wise guy.

Be helpful - offer help to someone in need. Let's see, if you turn it sideways, that way's North. No, you turn around, maybe that will work. Where's a tree? Look for moss.

Can you believe it. Some idiot today kept hollering, "Here Rudolph, Here Rudolph." I finally walked over and told him my name was Fred.

This group of hunters appears to be in silent meditation. Perhaps they are thinking about the days hunt, or it could be that it's been so long since they've seen a buck they're trying to remember what one looks like.

Occasionally help is required to remove whiskers stuck together with pancake syrup and venison gravy. There is evidently a chemical action that occurs after several days, and often there is no other way out.

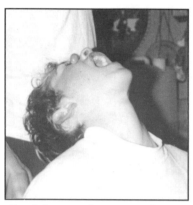

Teach the young hunter everyting you know. The olive catch is excellent practice for capturing errant snow flakes during a blizzard.

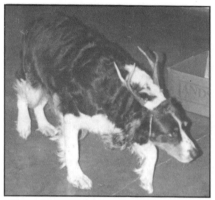

The tufelope makes an excellent creature to sharpen your tracking skills on, during off hours. A word of caution. Although at times they are successful, never count on fire hydrants as making the perfect stand.

This is a rare photo of the World Record Marsh Buck. In the words of this hunter, "I knew as soon as I had it in the scope, it was the largest marsh buck I'd ever seen." It was. The left nubbin measures 3/16", the right 1/8". Almost a perfectly matched rack. Behind that proud smile, the hunter of this trophy also states, "don't believe everything you see."

Don't ever be afraid to display your patriotism. These men have all signed up to join the naval forces. Actually, there was a debate as to which had the biggest belly. It would appear to me "No Contest."

Did you ever wonder why it doesn't bother a deer hunter to pick up a deer dropping, roll it between his fingers, and then pinch it to check its age, but at home he can't change a diaper?

Author's Note:I wish to thank the camp reporter, Al Kramschuster, and the "Buck's Lodge Crew" for allowing me to delve into their private journal to remove excerpts from their many hunts, in order that I might produce "The Buck's Lodge Camp Log."

In Al's very own words:

This is a camp diary of one deer hunting crew. It's members always come together or separately. It is a fairly factual account from 1975 until 1980. From 1981 on it will be kept current as the season progresses. Consequently the early years are vague in terms of anything other than deer shot. From 1981 on it will occupy a number of pages each season as we can better remember deer shot, missed, and seen.

NOTICE:

To all camp members: Do not write in this journal without prior approval from Al Kramschuster (Hoople) as I can make enough misteaks without your help.

Al Kramschuster

Opening Day Eve - Roll Call:

Alvin Henry Herman Buchholtz
Darrell Ervin Pagenkopf
William Alvin Buchholtz
Randy Joseph Carlson
Norbert Arthur Martin
Keith Alan Young
Hugh James Fleming
Alan Jon Kramschuster
John Michael Deminsky
Dana Dean Remillard
Rodney Allen Martin

The Friday night tradition is being upheld by 6:08. "The Two Who Tend to Tipple" have been here since about noon so you can draw your own conclusions. Alvie is in charge of the heat and it is a comfortable 91 degrees in here. Norbie said this is the worst crew he has ever hunted with. Randy and Hughie are talking business (boo - hiss). The "social hour" and "double bubble" are running concurrently this year from 5:00 p.m. to 1:00 a.m. Wet tonight - forecast is for a low of 36 and a high of 40 tomorrow with a 70% chance of rain tonight and 60% chance tomorrow.

Rod, Bill, John D., and Darrell have hunter's choice permits so we have 4 hunter's choice and 8 buck tags to fill. The DNR expects a 200,000 plus kill this year, but I don't think it will be that high.

Norb is cooking a moose roast that Norm Henneman gave to Rod. Norb forgot to thaw the moose so it went in the pot frozen. It will still be delicious when it's done at 9:00 or 10:00 or 11:00 or . . . . .

Randy brought some sausage (8#) and chops (5#) from a bear he shot this year and some salmon from the Kenai peninsula. Norb brought some muskie too.

Norb is really thinking about the squeaky mouse but hasn't got any cheese. Oh well - tomorrow is another day.

Day 1
Alarms off at 4:30. Bill is bound and determined to leave at 5:30 for his stand. It was raining hard but we all got ready to go. Temperature was 45°. The rain let up and we took off. Bill, Rod, Randy, John, and Al K. went back behind Beaver Lake and Alvie B., Norb, and Darrell went down on the land. The absolute BEST opening day we have ever had was about to start.

Randy went on landing #2 on the land and at 7:06½ a big buck came from the south along the tamaracks about 100 yards away. One shot and a huge 9 point was in the bag.

Darrell was sitting down on the south end of the land. At 6:30 a big buck came up behind him about 10 feet away. It was so dark that Darrell could only watch it go by. Then about 7:00 he saw two more but couldn't scope them for horns. Then at 7:26 Darrell nailed a 4 point with 3 shots. The buck almost ran him over.

Bill B. shot a 5 point (most guys would call it 4) at about 7:30. 3 shots. The buck had a big body for so few points. He hit it at least twice out of the three shots. Bill saw a doe and a fawn go down by the lake.

John got a 4 point at about 7:50. He hit it in the lungs and it ran about 200 yards. He went and gutted it and dragged it back to his stand, sat down, took two sips of pop, put his pop down, picked his gun up, and drilled a big-bodied 8 point.

Al K. heard John shoot the second time and John started yelling "Rod! Rod!" for Rod to come down and tag the buck. Al K. thought he was yelling "Buck! Buck" so he got ready and about 2 minutes later a buck came from John's direction, then turned and ran up to Al and he got a 7 point (most guys would call it 5) .

We had six bucks by 8:15!!! Rod saw 10 deer - all bald. Alvie saw nada. After we got the deer in we figured we'd go down and drive the land cause Norb was still standing on the south end. We drove it to the end and Rod jumped a buck but couldn't shoot right away cause Darrell was in the line of fire. Rod got a shot but missed and then Norb got a shot while the buck was going like a raped ape. Norb's still got it - one shot - one 4 point buck. SEVEN bucks on the pole. We had to put bucks on two hunter's choice tags.

Day 1 additions and corrections: Alvie saw a doe and two fawns but no tubing. Darrell saw two baldies about 1:00. Al K. and Bill saw a doe off Al's stand when they were dragging their bucks out.

Opening Day Night - Rod and John missed supper - some mysterious urge drove them to continue the pursuit on into the night. Darrell, the human tweezers, tried to remove a black hair from the end of Alvie's nose using only his teeth. He couldn't do it but liked trying so much that he tried a couple more times. Norb made another great supper. Muskie. He had a 16 pounder and a 35 incher he had to kill cause it had the bucktail way down in the gills. TERRIFIC! Al K. carried two bucks (one at a time—of course) up the A-frame hill yelling "I'm a man!" all the way. He must be in terrific shape. In fact, he's going to bed at 8:44 tonight to make sure he stays that way. Bill and Alvie are already in bed. Everyone else is out hoping a deer will run by a tavern and shooting today's bucks over and over and over and over.

Day 2
Weather today was there alright—yup—we had weather all day. In fact the weather was right out there in the woods. Great day today with lots of weather. Whether you like it or not.

Bill, Rod, and John went around Beaver Lake while Al, Dana, Hugh, and Norb went on stands. John saw 2, Rod saw 3, and Bill saw 4. Bill got a shot at a nice buck but it wasn't a good shot. About 100 yards through brush. Dana had a tough shot at a fork buck - about 20 yards away and walking right in front of him. He shot three times all around it and the buck walked off snickering to itself. Who says those deer aren't smart—that one knew just who to walk by. We checked by Dana's stand for empty shells.

We went down and put some logs across the logging road on our land and Bill's field road as too many people were driving in there without permission. Hopefully they will at least ask first from now on. Tried to catch a couple of trespassers on our land but no luck. We're pretty sure who it was and they won't be allowed down there again. We hung two bucks and a doe today.

There was a beautiful cat named Morris that came to the camp and all the hunters loved and fed him table scraps. But old Morris got greedy and started eating too much venison from the meat pole. This made the hunters very unfriendly. One hunter shot poor old Morris and that's old Morris hanging on the meat pole.

<u>Day 3</u>

Darrell shot a spike from Norb's tree stand. It took him two shots as he shot a tree first to confuse the deer and then shot it through the boiler room.

Norb saw his first deer of the day. It was a spike and after it took a dump Norb shot it. He's such a polite man. The spike dropped in its "tracks" at 30½ yds.

Garf shot a 5½ pt. in the front shoulder. Correction - Al K. a.k.a. "Eagle Eye Hoople" recounted the points. He spotted another point so Garf's buck is a legitimate 6 pt. The buck just came feeding down the snowmobile trail minding his own business when Garf cracked him.

Norbie saw a rare blue dove-tailed chicken hawk. John said "That ain't no chicken hawk, boy." Back to the shack at 11:00. I had forgotten, yesterday afternoon some kid tried to kick Darrell off his own stand. Darrell pretended he was deaf when the kid talked to him. The kid waved his arms and talked trying to get Darrell to leave. Darrell just sat there and the kid went wandering off muttering to himself.

Drove the land this afternoon—saw three. Rainy and miserable. It's getting colder and the wind is picking up—maybe a little snow, 4:59 and a little game of "31" with Al, Norb, Keith, and Hugh. We got in late because we made a drive to Keith and Randy but delayed getting to their stand for about two hours as punishment for missing their bucks.

Time for a little work on our hunter success statistics. From 1975 through 1987 (13 years) we have had 129 hunters who have bagged 71 bucks and 29 does/hunter's choice. The ratio of buck to doe kills is 71%. Our hunter success rate for bucks only is 55%. Our overall hunter success rate is 78%. Not bad for a bunch of government workers and an insurance salesman.

Day 4

It's horns only today so on the first drive Garf shot Bambette (Bambi's sister). Seven deer went by him and he shot the smallest one. He bare-eyed all of them except the one he shot. That one he used the scope on and it looked bigger in the scope. He was using .243 and wanted a pair of gloves for his boy so he didn't want to shoot too big a deer and waste any deerhide. After all the smart talk about shooting somebody's pet was over and done with we tied the deer to a fishpole and trolled for muskies for awhile. Then we put it in Bill's gun case and carried it out. When we got to the car we put it in the glove compartment and brought it back to the shack. We left it alone while we made a few more drives and it was still here when we got back although we were afraid "a cat might come along and drag it away. We got it hung up and tied a little pink ribbon and a bow on it. Lunch for all and a nap for some. It's 1:00 p.m. and the debate is on as to where to go. Made some drives in the flowages this afternoon. Saw a lot of deer but no horns. Bill saw a "possible" but couldn't be sure so no more deer hanging. So far we have seven on the pole with two hunter's choice to fill. We are a little short-handed but we have 5 days to go so maybe we'll get a buck or two yet.

Day 5 - Wednesday

Rod had two fawns pretty close to him and then he whistled and talked to them. They came up to about 20 feet from him and then just walked away. He shot the two bucks about 5 seconds apart as the big 9 pt. was following the smaller buck.

Drove Dumpling Lake and the Death Trap in the afternoon but no deer. Keith and Norb hunted in the afternoon and decided to scout out the island at the end of the Death Trap. They saw two beds—one was a twin sized with brass headboard and the other was a queen size waterbed. Keith made his foot disappear through the ice on his way out from the scouting expedition. Back to the cottage for cards and a great supper of ribs, dumplings, and sauerkraut. A few card games and in the rack early as we all plan on standing for Thanksgiving morning. Should be a good day to stand as the weather is changing and there will be a lot of hunters moving around tomorrow. Norb really had something to Crow about tonight as he spit in his drink and drank from his spit cup.

Bill and Darrell are establishing a new distance record for an olive toss. Bill is tossing them from the sink and Darrell is out by the screen door on the porch and catching them in his mouth. 34 feet! Played two games of 31 tonight for $3.00 each to get in. Rod won a game and Dana won a game— $18.00 each. Needless to say they each had to buy a round at "Lyin' Don's." Dana sent the money but couldn't go along to enjoy.

Winter Storm watch for tomorrow—Thanksgiving Day.

Day 6

Thanksgiving Day—Rod, Bill, Norb, Darrell, and John went on stands. Rod and Darrell went out late and Rod shot an 8 point in the same spot Bill got the buck with his bow. It was raining and they were just poking along when the buck came around the pond on the south side. They both opened up—Darrell shot once and Rod shot 4 times. They both hit the deer in the same place as there was only one entry hole—Good Shooting—Huh?"

Down to the land this afternoon and made a couple of drives. Saw a lot of deer and we got an ID on all of them except two. Ran into Clyde and he invited us down to his woods tomorrow so we'll go down there about midday and try it. Norb came back up for turkey and if he stays well he might be able to finish the season with us.

Turkey and all the trimmings for supper. We'll have to start calling Garf "Hughie" but then he'd probably quit cooking. A little wait for the pie as we had a fire in the oven after we took the turkey out.

Day 7

Everybody up today—even John. He's still looking pretty weasel-eyed. It's time to shoot another buck as we've been dry since Monday. Maybe someone will crack Bambi's big brother. Drove the land north—saw 3. Drove Ronnie's—saw zip. Back for lunch and a nap.

Polock scores on a 5 point off the popple knob at about noon. He jumped and he had to run across thin ice to get a shot.

Norb, Bill, and Al went back behind Dumpling Lake. Bill jumped a big deer but no horns. Bill drove the Death Trap and saw one. Al saw 2 and Norb thinks he saw either a fox or a squirrel. Squirrels are the little gray ones and fox are the medium-size red ones. He saw a movement of some kind—bowel—pincer—left-face—right-face—musical—or something.

Day 8

Made the Beaver Lake drive this morning where all the deer were seen yesterday. Moved two little ones past Darrell but he didn't shoot. 3 degrees this morning but clear and got up into the mid-20s in the afternoon. Rod shot a "nice" doe this afternoon east of Dumpling Lake. Rod is now the DDCDS (Designated Deer Camp Doe Slayer).

Deer seen for the season so far:

Darrell	19	John	19	Bill	12
Norb	12	Al K.	4		
Rod	26	Alvie	3		
Dana	15	Randy	6	TOTAL	106

Rod did the dishes and Al picked up while Norb slept. Bill, John, and Dana went over to the flowages to pick up some stuff on their stands. Made a couple of drives in the afternoon over in the flowages with no luck.

Day 9 - The Last Day

Polack had two bucks walk by him in the morning off Norbie's stand behind Beaver Lake. Both had spikes but he thought one was too small so he shot the other. It turned out be a 4 point. The one he let go by was probably legal also.

Notes - Darrell found a dead beaver. It had chewed off a tree and the tree slipped off the stump and pinned the beaver's tail to the ground. The beaver starved to death.

Waiting for Alvie to get here so we can load the deer and take them to Ronnie's to register them.

Cleaned up the cabin and skinned and cut up deer at Hoople's. All done by 3:30. Thanks Buck for the use of the cabin again. We couldn't have a better place to hunt from or a better crew to hunt with. The years to come will be even better as the boys start to hunt and have fun with us.

Opening Camp #2

The eve of opening day - Friday night -

Who's here you ask?

		Age
Old Crew	- Alvin Buchholtz	70
	- Norb Martin	57
	- Rod Martin	30
	- Bill Buchholtz	30
	- Keith Young	23
	- Al Kramschuster	34
	- Darrell Pagenkopf	31
	- John Diminski	32
	- Gary Kramschuster	31
	- Hugh Fleming	25 - (Huey,

Dewey, Louie, Bigfoot, Captain Crunch, Gentle Ben in Heat)

Tradition was once again upheld as "The Two Who Tend to Tipple" had a noseful by suppertime on the eve of opening day. One had gotten a little Weasel-eyed, the other stayed white-eyed. Both were tucked in bed by 6:17 p.m.

Garf, Al, and Norb were here at 2:30 to get supper ready and peel potatoes over at Don's. John is back on his rifle stand or should I say "by his rifle stand." A big oak fell on it and it's trapped. Lucky for him Bill and Al took pity on him and walked back to the stand and lifted the tree off "Wimpy's" stand. This will now be called the "The Polack Decathlon."

We had to cut the neck roast we were having for supper with a bow saw as it was slightly frozen. It's in the oven now so we have to preview the movies and then go to Don's to peel the potatoes.

Bill brought 3 boxes of snuff for the whole season. He must plan on ending the season about 11:00 tonight. He set the camp record. It's not a camp record anyone else envies as he has made 5 trips to the outhouse so far—and it's only 8:30. Norb spit in his drink already tonight so he's on track for a successful season.

Another camp record was established, as Norb sneezed 14 times in a row. We thought he was a goner after 13.

Ate the neck roast and headed for bed.

Opening Day

Up and at 'em early. Norb, Darrell, and Garf down to the land. Bill, Rod, Al, John, and Dana back on stands in the flowages. Norb shot a 6 pt. at 7:15. He is definitely going to charge rent next year. He also shot another buck at about 2:30 that ran onto the neighbor's posted land and shortly after he heard a shot and someone yell "It's a buck!," so we lost one. John shot a big 6 pt. at 6:43 and a 5 pt. at 7:48. He should be grateful to Bill and Al.

If they wouldn't have lifted the tree off his stand he may not have shot those two bucks. He did buy them a drink although that wasn't much of a gesture as he used the shack "kitty" to do it.

Keith Young shot a fork buck early in the morning. Al K. and Rod could hear his whoop from their stands. It was a 3-toed buck. Hoople—Al K.—shot a nice doe (nobody ever shoots a doe that isn't "nice") in the morning after taking a shot at a buck following a doe and missing.

Bill had another buck hit hard that ran behind him and a twelve year old kid shot at it and hit it. Rod took the blood trail but gave the buck to the kid as it was his first buck. Everybody in bed early tonight after all the deer dragging today.

<u>Day 2</u>
Warm again.
Alvie Buchholtz—nubbin buck/party tag.
Al Kramschuster and Rod Martin messed up on a spike buck. They were sitting on Hoople's stand about 11:30 and had a party tag to fill. Al K. saw 3 deer and wanted to shoot the doe. At the same time Rod saw another deer and said Al should shoot it because it was a big doe. Then the "big doe" whirled and ran off as Rod sees the spikes and fires and misses. Al never got his tube off.

Alvie shot a "nice" doe. Our two hunter's choice permits are now filled with doe, so it's bucks only from now on.

Back to the shack at 4:00 for a little game of 31 and supper. Keith saw a duck come in for a landing by the beaver dam at Kelly's but surprise for the duck as there was no water but a lot of ice. The duck just skidded across the ice and then sat there with an embarrassed look on his bill. Keith laughed his ass off but it appears there is still plenty there.

Oh, did I forget to mention Rod shot a 6 month old doe. These are commonly known in hunting vernacular as fawns, bambettes, sub-adults, antlerless deer, hunter's choice, golded retrievers, small dogs, mulies, jackrabbits, and "big lone deer."

<u>Day 3</u>
Alvie & Hugh went down on the land. Hugh saw two flags. Everybody else went over to the flowages on stands. Dana saw 6—no horns. John saw 1—spike buck at 6:44 a.m.—one shot through the base of the neck and pulped the heart. Rod shot a 5½ point at 12:00. It took him four shots to get it as he shot two trees and hit the deer twice. Bill shot a big racked 6 point at 12:50 (13" inside spread). He saw five deer at the same time and three of them were bucks. He shot and missed the first one, then got the 6 point, and then missed a spike. He also banged himself right between the eyes with the scope.

Al K. shot a 10 point (12¾" inside spread) at 1:45 p.m. It was following a doe and never knew what hit it. He was fortunate to even be in the woods as he tore the shack apart looking for his backtag in the morning. Then after he found his backtag he accused his good hunting buddies of taking his gun because he pulled his case out of the truck and it had Keith's gun in it. Turned out it was Keith's case that he checked and his own was right in front of him all the time.

Norbie got a wet hinder on the way back to the shack today. Keith and Al slid a buck across some thin ice and then they walked down and crossed on the beaver dam. Norbie (the old Indian and trail sign reader) followed the drag trail across the thin ice and fell in. Four bucks to take up "Heartbreak Hill."

Day 4
Made the same drive behind Beaver Lake that we made yesterday. Saw 2 before the drive started. Then Bill saw a buck and a doe. Couldn't get a shot at the buck. Norb saw four—John saw 3—Rod saw 2—Dana saw one—Keith saw 3—Al saw 3. Al K. shot a "magnum" doe with his 50 caliber muzzleloader. Broke her back at 60 yards. About 15 minutes later he missed a buck with the old pumpkin-slinger—tough shot—just saw head and back running flat out at 60 yds.

Then drove the elbow. Hugh saw 1—Al K. saw 3—one was a buck with stubbed horns—not legal—I think. Dinner time at 2:30. Al had to unload his muzzleloader by shooting it so Norb threw his $8.00 hat in the air. When the smoke cleared there was a hole in Norb's hat—50 cal. in size.

Three bald-headed deer on the "Death Trap" and four bald ones past Norb out of Snyder's.

The hunter's choice could have been filled today. Norb will need a new safety on his rifle cause he said he had it on and off so much today that it's wearing out! 14 deer seen today—Alvie says there's no deer around but 5 guys moved 14 today. Norbie thinks he's making supper and Polack is going out tonight. Keith shot a tree on the slim excuse that he bumped his scope—I think he just wanted to get his tube off.

Day 5

Warmer today and partly cloudy. Bill, Norb, John, and Garf here this morning and Al to get here after lunch. Made a few drives this morning and then when driving out the boys saw a buck standing by the boat landing. A mad scramble ensued with John and Norb getting their guns out. Norb knocked Bill's gun on the ground so he couldn't shoot. The buck escaped.

We drove the back half of the land. Moved 6 or 7 baldies around but no horns. Hoople saw 4 off the beaver dam stand this morning. Back to the shack and on stands this afternoon. Garf saw 2 and John saw 1. Everybody else saw woods. We plan on cranking one on Thanksgiving Day morning.

Cards this afternoon and then all the young boys are up here for the night. Josh, Jamie, Adam, Eric, and Mike get a taste of camp life tonight and some hunting in the morning. John shot a partridge off the ground today too. He shot it right in the neck on his second shot. Drove the Popple Knob and kicked eight off it.

The rest of us are still trying. John is going to try the borrowed equipment ruse tomorrow and Darrell is trying the whining ruse in hopes of bagging a buck tomorrow. The rest of us are going to sit in Norb's, Jamie's, Adam's, and Garf's back pockets.

Pretty quiet shack life. Hoople took $6.00 off Jamie shaking dice. Rod went to town but was back by 10:30 claiming he took a hot bath. Lights out about 9:00 for the rest of us.

Day 6

Garf and Norb up early to put the turkey in, then we went and made four drives. Warm today with temp supposed to hit 50 and sunny. Saw six deer and then back to the shack for turkey. Probably go to Al's tonight and skin the deer.

Turkey and no deer!

Day 7

Went back to the flowages today and stood until 8:30 and then made a couple of drives. Saw a lot of deer but no horns. We went to Clyde's and made two drives. Bill, Garf, and Al drove without their rifles. A 4 pt. jumped out of the woods between Norb and John. Norb shot it. For a minute we thought we'd have to hire an arbitrator to decide who shot it but John said Norb hit it. Al gutted it for Norb so now Norb owes him two guts.

Took all the deer to Hoople's to skin and quarter. We worked from 9:30 to about 3:30 so all we have left is to cut and wrap the meat. Hoople counted coup on a doe this morning with his truck. The doe and the truck went down the road side-by-side until the deer bumped the side of the truck. Then we slowed down and let the deer cross the road. Big feed of tenderloin and onions tonight.

Day 8

Rod shot a "mule" deer at 10:15 a.m. He gelded it. It was a 4 pt. with three points on one side and a broken horn on the other side. The third side didn't have any points as there are only two sides you drunk. Josh shot a 3 pt. at 7:09:30 plus one. He is 12 years old so it's only fair that he should shoot a 3 pt. Don't ask me why but it just seems fair. Darrell shot a doe at 3:30 p.m. She was getting venisoned by a buck when he shot her. I don't know why he didn't shoot the buck—perhaps he'll die.

Well, well, well—Keith got his gun off this morning. We drove the south side of White's field and north of Dumpling Lake to the east. Moved 9 deer and Keith saw 5 of them. He was on the south end of Dumpling Lake by the shack when they came through. The fifth one had horns (3 pt.) and Keith broke its back at 35 yards on the run. He shot at it three more times because its eyelids were still twitching. Needless to say we had to check his pants and then get him quieted down enough to put a tag on it.

Everybody cleaned up their bodies—which is a rare treat around here—and then sat around watching the TV. It's 4:00 p.m. and just R and R until tonight.

Day 9

Up and at 'em bright and early this morning at 8:30. John made a big breakfast. Darrell had a good time with a flyswatter last night and Bill got in a fight with a barstool and went down for the seven-count. He got right back up and toughed it out until 1:00 a.m. Norb leaked out at 11:00 p.m. cause he started too early.

Not many crews around that enjoy the success and the good times that we do here. Brought in some new blood this year too as Josh (Bill's boy), Eric (Darrell's boy), and Adam (Garf's boy) spent a little time with us. They saw some deer and Josh saw a buck on a drive we made without guns just to see if the boys could see a deer. Next year they may be hunting with us so we'll have to teach them how to drag out deer. It takes a lot of practice and hopefully we'll provide them with ample opportunity to learn.

Picture time and cleanup. Just around shooting deer from years past. Now it's to Ronnie's and registration and the party's over.

They just keep getting better and better.

Opening Camp #3

The crew this year:

Bill Buchholtz	
Josh Buchholtz	
Jamie Buchholtz	
Rod Martin	- hunter's choice
Norb Martin	- hunter's choice
Al Kramschuster	- hunter's choice
Gary Kramschuster	- hunter's choice
Dana Remillard	- hunter's choice
Darrell Pagenkopf	- hunter's choice
John Deminske	
Eric Pagenkopf	
Adam Kramschuster	
(card player)	

Twelve of us this year as Alvie, Hugh, and Keith won't be here this year. Alvie figured he couldn't do it anymore as he's 76. He shot a lot of deer in his day and a couple of big racks are hanging on the porch to prove it. His last couple of years up here weren't the best for him as he couldn't get around very good and couldn't hunt the way he used to. I suppose there will come a day all of us must make this same decision. Everybody is a year older and from the sound of things around here everybody got a year smarter. Of course you may still believe in the tooth fairy.

Now that Alvie doesn't hunt anymore there will be an election to determine who the oldest hunter is. Norbie is one of the candidates but nobody here will vote for him. The problem with a "Norbie" presidency is there won't be a safe push anywhere. Another problem will be trying to understand him when he starts talking "cowboy." He should do well in the Western states. Garf is running also but Norb is trying to steal his ideas. Garf's main platform is "a chick in every bed" or "a chicken in every pot" or "a bed in every bedroom" or "a bath in every bathroom" or "a bear in every den" or "a TV in every car" or "a Hoople in everything." I'll vote for that! Another candidate is obviously losing his mind—he thinks he's a lesbian because he likes women.

Most of us were smart enough to eat and hit the sack early. See you in the morning. It's the opener.

Opening Day

33 with a cold breeze and damp. Norb, Josh, Jamie, Darrell, and Eric are going down to the land. The rest of us are going to the flowages. Bill and Rod left at 5:28. They're taking Rod's 4-wheeler to the landing and then in from there. We didn't see a lot of deer bowhunting but the sign was there. A lot of people are feeding deer year-round so maybe they aren't moving as much or all the standing corn is holding them—we hope. It couldn't possibly be that the DNR screwed up and issued too many hunter's choice last year and overestimated the deer herd. No way—they go out and count deer pellets which everyone knows is an extremely accurate way to tell where the deer are crapping. A report goes to a DNR Manager that says "deer are crapping in huge amounts here." That Manager then sends a report to his boss that says "huge amounts of deer are crapping here." Finally the DNR board receives a report that says "There are huge amounts of crapping deer" and thus hunter's choice permits and bonus tags are issued in huge amounts.

As I reread a sentence above I notice I stated "We didn't see a lot of deer bowhunting. It's too hard for them to hold the arrow on the rest with just their hoof.

Jamie started it off at 8:00 with a 4 pt. corn-fed buck shot right in the base of the neck. The buck came from the "Pink Carpet" to "The Ditch Stand." Jamie had a 20 yd. shot and the buck just flew over backwards and was a goner. This is Jamies' first buck shot with a rifle so he's a happy Willard.

Adam shot a doe right in the heart at 25 yds. This is the first full-size deer he has shot. He played it smart and let the doe walk by him and when she looked away—Adam greased her. He may want to remember that technique on any future dates. He gutted the deer himself so he's on his own from now on. He made a nice shot on a nice doe.

Bill shot a beautiful even-racked 8 pt. at 7:00. It was following four does and had already run out of luck as it went by Jamie at 30 yards but the Rat hadn't put a shell in the chamber so he just practiced aiming and the buck ran past Dad. The buck had a 13 and 5/8" inside spread and Bill figures on having it mounted to go on his wall with the big buck he shot with the bow a few years back.

Darrell, Garf, Norb, and Al all missed bucks today. Darrell missed a one-horn buck, Norb missed a spike, Garf missed a spike, and Al missed a spike. We all screwed up one way or another.

Snowy, windy, and miserable all day. Some of us stuck it out until 3:30 or so but the deer weren't moving unless someone kicked them out.

Day 2

Rod shot a spike today. It may have been a 6 pt. but its horns were all busted up and it only had parts of the main tines left. He shot it about 9:00 after another guy had jumped it and missed it three times. The buck was running by Rod and then it turned and ran right at him and he kilt it right on the logging road.

Adam popped a buck fawn this morning. He shot three times and we won't have conclusive results on where and how many times he hit it until after the autopsy. Let's just say it took some mighty fine shooting to hit a target that small. It was tough shooting too because the fawn kept hiding behind twigs and it really got tough as some of those twigs had a leaf or two left on them.

10:15 a.m. - Garf shot an 8 pt. that came along the east side of the pothole. He had a few shooting openings and then the buck stopped behind some trees. He took one step out and Garf shot him through both front shoulders. He dropped on the spot.

Unusual items: The deer was bigger than the one Garf shot last year and it didn't have a ribbon on it. It didn't blow out of the truck and he used 40 lb. test line instead of 10 lb. test to troll for muskies. It was not easily confused with a squirrel. An autopsy later revealed the buck was shot in the neck not the front shoulders—Garf's sight must have been off—right?

7:15 a.m. - John D. Polack shot a 7 pt. It was the 18th deer he saw. It came from the east down the hill. He hit it the first shot, missed the second, and probably missed the third. He took the top of the heart off and blew up the lungs. The buck ran about 30 yards and slowed to a walk and then dropped.

10:00 a.m. - Bill shot a 5-1/16 point that he saw laying in its bed. It may have been there all morning as the blankets were all messed up and its dirty underwear were still at the bottom of the bed. Bill hit him straight on in the neck and the buck just went back to sleep. Deer seen - 30.

Unusual items. The buck had a golf-ball size tumor on the inside of its left back leg. There was an alarm clock in its bed and a Hustler magazine.

The deer Darrell shot was a credit to Darrell's keen eyesight and is a serious threat to Garf's record for the camp bambette. It's a good thing the snowshoe bunnies are turning white now so Darrell could tell this was a deer. Josh dragged it out but he said it hardly touched the ground when he pulled it. This deer was so small we call it our "Dangerfield" deer cause it don't get no respect. This deer was so small when we hung it on the pole the sag went <u>out</u> of the pole. This deer was so small only chickadees came to the gutpile. This deer was so small we field-dressed it with a finger-nail clipper. This deer was so small we'll have to cook it in a micro wave. This deer was so small it dragged faster uphill than it did downhill. This deer was so small Darrell could be arrested for infanticide. This deer was so small Darrell had to take its diaper off to field-dress it. This deer was so small it never turned a leaf or left a trail when Josh dragged it out. This deer was so small a squirrel was following it with lust on his mind. This deer was so small when Rod butchered it he had to cut half-minute steaks. This deer was so small we cut it in half to get two quarters. And finally, this deer was so small even Garf thought it was small.

Garf, Adam, Bill, Jamie, Eric, Rod, and Al here today. Up and out early today and made two drives on our land. Drove the front half first and Bill shot a big dog coyote down by the beaver dam. It ran by him just as Bill came over the knob by "Partridge Rock." Drove the back half and kicked some deer out. We could have shot plenty of does this morning but didn't. There was a deer bedded down again today where Al and Jamie shot their does. They seem to like that spot.

Day 4
Garf and Darrell relinquished their rights to claim the smallest deer ever shot up here. Adam now holds that record. He has a 1½ to 4½ scope and he says he had it on 4½ when he shot the deer. I guess we can be glad he didn't have a 9 power or we would have had to put a tag on a squirrel. As it is we aren't too sure if we tagged a squirrel or not.

Oink-Oink! Al the Hoople shot two bucks at 8:30 this morning. They were traveling together. His first shot dropped the lead buck in his tracks and the second buck jumped back a few bounds. Hoople shot again and the buck tottered out of sight. Al went and called Garf and John and two bucks were in the bag. Speed-gut record also set as Al gutted both bucks in a total of 13 minutes including travel time between them.

One didn't get past Josh. Some guys will do anything to get their name in the camp journal. Josh said "It's a fawn and I'm proud of it." Jamie and Adam went over to see it and did see it—as soon as they brushed a couple of leaves aside. John and Al went over to see it and did see it—as soon as they lifted Josh's gloves off it. It was a twin to the one Rod shot in the bow season—although I think this one was the premature twin. A little smaller and it would have been a miscarriage.

Day 5

The weatherman finally got a forecast right. That's the good news. The bad news is that the forecast was for RAIN!!! It started raining at 6:30 a.m. and rained until 1:00 p.m. Even with that we did pretty good. Bill shot a 3½ point at 7:23. It came up alongside him about 10 yards away and walked by him and then he dropped it. All he saw at first was a horn moving along like a puppet on a string. Hugh shot a "perfect" spike at 7:00 on the dot. He had seen it well before he shot but wasn't sure it was a buck or doe.

We drove the Dumpling Lake knob and the slashings and found a dead 6 point. The buck had been dead for quite awhile—at least a couple of weeks. Tomorrow we plan on propping up the dead buck we found and seeing how many goofy roadhunters stop and take a shot at it.

Adam wrote in the journal without permission but he's forgiven cause he was a little excited after winning 10 games of buck euchre.

The boys stayed over last night so the spots are getting worn off the cards. They're all winning money so it's just like Las Vegas around here. Nobody ever goes to Vegas and loses—they all either win or break even. Early to bed as tomorrow we're going to fill that buck tag of Jim's.

Day 6 - Turkey Day!
Very windy—raw and cold. Drove Dumpling Lake, our land, and the flowages. Saw a lot of deer but wanted the boys to shoot so we passed on a few. Saw a bear walking in to the flowages to make a drive—almost everybody saw it except Hoople and Adam. Adam proceeded to get lost in the elbow. He put a lot of miles on but came out to the lake. He stayed put until he heard John yell for him and then he thought maybe John was lost too. They both got out and we're back at the shack with "lost" stories and "bear" stories flying around.

Raining cats, dogs, pitchforks, horseapples, and anything else you can think of. Can't get to go—raining too hard. Forecast is for rain turning to snow today and winter storm watch for tomorrow. Some of the boys went road hunting and some went shopping. Big poker game today. Bill went out in the rain for about one hour. He jumped 3 big deer right behind Ed's place but couldn't tell what they were. Started to snow at 3:00 p.m. and windy.

We feasted on a meal of turkey and all the goodies. One thing that should go on record is the fact we have yet to lose a man in camp due to starvation.

Day 7
7:00 - Drove the slashings—Rod let a doe and two fawns go by. Drove the land, Burroughs, Kelly's, and Winkie's till noon. Nada except John shot three times at an invincible fox (Reginald, Fleetfoot, HA, Fox). After lunch we drove behind Popple Knob. Bill got a wet hinder as he fell in—gun and all.

His backstroke needs a little polishing. Drove the slashing again—nothing. Getting late in the day and still need a doe and 3 bucks. Started a drive between the lakes and Rod stayed back at the bottom of the land. Boom - Boom—Rod shot a "nice" doe going across the ice.

Chuck "The Rifleman" Fleming tried to shoot a doe at 20 yards. Emptied his gun but no blood. Randy's doe was a "perfect" doe. Hughie dulled all his knives gutting out deer today. Hunter's choice are filled and the day is done. It's Miller Time!!! Everybody is beat—most in bed by 8:30. Darrell won $9.00 from Dana playing "31" and in bed by 11:00.

Six to twelve inches of snow forecast for tonight so we took the deer in and registered them. Back to the shack.

Day 8 - Saturday

There's about 2 inches of heavy wet snow on the ground and it's falling steadily so it looks like the season could be over. We haven't filled Dana's hunter's choice tag but not because we couldn't. We just wanted to be able to hunt a little longer. Everyone is getting their stuff together and Norb is cooking up a big breakfast. Winter storm watch for tonight and tomorrow. Forecast is for 6-12 inches tonight so today may be our last day of fairly easy walking. There is over 15 inches of snow in the woods now and any more will make it rough going. Now the snow is powdery because of the cold. A mystery man dampened our porch last night from inside the screen door. Even Norb the party animal is ready to head home.

Day 9

A BLIZZARD! Lots of snow falling and everybody up and packed and on the road home by 9:00. Left the shack dirty and will clean it up later in the week and this season is history. Rod and Bill are licking their wounds yet from last night. The rest of us didn't drink a drop. Another great year as we saw a ton of deer and our hunter success rate was 100%. Can it get any better than this?

The young boys will remember their early hunting years all their lives and hopefully turn into as great of guys as their dads and their hunting buddies are.

HUNTER HINT { Plan your days hunt to keep the sun on your back. }

You Got It!
You Fix It!

These are the very words often heard by successful hunters as they return home from the hunt, their valiant effort to keep food on the table for their families fulfilled.

Here are some proven recipes to use that will let you, as a hunter, not only practice the cooking skills you used in camp, but will enable you to create culinary delights beyond your wildest imagination. (If you believe all this, I have a beautiful ocean side lot with sandy beach for sale near Weyerhaeuser Wisconsin.)

Recipe #1

If you, at one time or another, have dined on poorly pre-pared venison, this is the recipe for you. It is an excellent way in which to confuse the eater. Once your subjects are unable to detect the difference between venison and beef, you will be in complete control.

We thank Barron County Agent Don Drost for contribut-ing this culinary tidbit, the venison-beef taste test.

Drost reports that the venison-beef taste test began by lead-ing a high-choice Holstein steer into a swamp a mile and a half from the nearest road and then shooting it several times. After some of the entrails were removed, the carcass was dragged over rocks and logs, through mud and dust, thrown into a pickup box and transported through rain and snow 100 miles before being hung out in the sun for 10 days.

After that, the steer was lugged to a garage, skinned and rolled around on the floor. Strict sanitary precautions were observed within the limitations of the butchering environment. For instance, dogs and cats were allowed to sniff at the steer carcass, but were chased out of the garage if they attempted to lick the carcass, bite it or sit on the workbench.

The steer was then dragged into the house and down the basement steps where half a dozen enthusiastic, though inex-perienced, butchers waited with meat saws, cleavers and dull knives. The result, a couple of hours later, was 375 pounds of soup bones, 4 bushels of meat scraps and a couple of steaks that were and eighth of an inch thick on one edge and an inch and a half on the other.

The steaks were fried in a skillet full of rancid bacon grease, along with 3 pounds of onions. After 2 hours of frying, the contents of the skillet were served to three blindfolded taste-test volunteers. All three thought the meat was venison. One of the tasters even said that it tasted exactly like the venison he had eaten at hunting camps for the past 27 years.

The results proved conclusively that there is no difference between the taste of beef and venison.

Seriously, the following recipes are tried and proven. Try them, you'll like them.

Barbecued Round of Venison

4 Tbs. bacon drippings	1½ large onion
½ cup celery	½ clove garlic minced
¼ cup vinegar	½ tsp. dry mustard
½ tsp. chili powder	1-½ tsp. salt
¼ tsp. pepper	1-½ Tbsp. sugar
1 cup tomato juice	½ cup water
1 five-ounce can tomato paste	

Cut a 1- inch thick slice of venison round into 4 pieces, dredge in flour and brown in bacon drippings or other shortening in deep skillet. Add onion coarsely chopped, chopped celery and clove garlic. Simmer 5 minutes longer.

Into vinegar dissolve dry mustard, chili powder, salt, pepper and sugar. Pour over venison along with water, tomato juice and tomato paste. Cover skillet tightly and simmer 2 hours, adding small amount of water as necessary.

The sauce makes excellent gravy just as it is for mashed potatoes.

Venison Stew

3 pounds venison cubed fried in butter	2 small cans tomato paste
3 leeks, cut up	8 Tbls. olive oil
4 cloves garlic	2 large cans pitted black olives, sliced
2 tsp. oregano	2 red peppers seeded and cut in strips
½ bottle hearty red wine	

Heat oil and simmer leeks, peppers and garlic until soft. Add oregano, tomato paste and wine. Simmer until tasty and add venison and sliced olives. Layer over cooked lasagna noodles. Top with grated Parmesan cheese, if desired.

Venison Roast

3 pounds venison	3 Tbls. flour
1 cup onion chopped	3 Tbls. red wine
4 slices bacon	Salt and pepper
1 red pepper or dash of red pepper	

Cook venison until tender in water. Add salt and pepper. Cool. Cut into small pieces and put in pan and cover with the stock it was cooked in. Put onion, flour, wine and bacon strips on top. Cook for 2 hours in low oven.

Venison Swiss Steak

1½ pounds venison cut into ½ inch pieces	2 cloves of garlic minced
12 ounce can tomato sauce or spaghetti sauce	4 Tbls. oil or butter
1 medium onion diced	½ cup flour
1 green pepper diced	½ tsp. salt
	¼ tsp. pepper
	¼ tsp. oregano

Saute onion, pepper and garlic until soft not brown. Mix flour, salt and pepper in a paper or plastic bag; put in venison and shake to coat meat. Remove and brown in oil. Layer meat and vegetables into a casserole or an oven bag. Cover with sauce and bake in a 350 degree oven for 1½ hours. Serve over spaghetti or rice. Another variation: Slice and saute 6 ounces of mushrooms instead of green pepper. Use 1 can cream of mushroom soup and ½ cup milk instead of tomato sauce. Serve with noodles.

Venison Chili

3 pounds venison, ground or small cubes	1 tsp. salt
	6 large onions
1 tsp. tabasco sauce	4 large green peppers
2 Tbls. chili powder	1 dozen red peppers
1 Tbls. Cumin	5 chili peppers
1 tsp. cayenne pepper	1 can red kidney beans
2 cans tomato sauce	1 can white beans
10 cloves garlic	

Brown venison, green peppers and onions in large heavy skillet. Add all ingredients except beans and simmer 45 minutes. Add beans with juice and simmer 15 minutes more.

Venison Stroganoff

1 pound ground meat	1 Tbls. sherry
½ cup minced onion	¼ tsp. each salt and pepper
1 stalk celery, minced	1 Tbls. butter
½ cup fresh mushrooms, chopped	½ pound mushrooms, sliced
	2 cups sour cream
3 cloves garlic, minced	¼ tsp. Worchestershire
2 or 3 Tbls. mince parsley	sauce

Mix together meat, 1/4 cup of minced onions, celery,

Mix together meat, 1/4 cup of minced onions, celery, chopped mushrooms, 2/3 of the garlic, salt and pepper. Shape into 1-inch balls. In a large frying pan over medium heat, saute meatballs 5 minutes. Drain fat. Add butter, sliced mushrooms, remaining onion and remaining garlic and saute 5 minutes more. Stir in sour cream, reduce heat and simmer until sauce is heated through, about 5 minutes.

Deer In A Bag

5 lbs. roast, shoulder or loin	2 onions sliced
1 can onion soup	½ lb. bacon
1 can of mushrooms	1 oven cooking bag
1 bottle Italian dressing	2 tablespoons flour

In a bag, marinate meat in Italian dressing. Leave in refrigerator overnight. Before cooking, remove excess dressing and add 1 tablespoon of flour to marinated mixture in the bag and shake. Place sliced onions around roast and cover meat with raw strips of bacon. Pour soup and mushrooms into the bag and tie the bag closed. Poke a few holes in the top of the bag. Roast in a pan at 280 degrees for 45 minutes for each pound of meat. Drain drippings into a sauce pan and heat, adding flour to make a thick rich gravy.

Jack Pine Steak

Most any cut of venison will work well, but do not use round, for it tends to be tough.

Remove all fat and fiber. Cut steaks 3/8 to 1/2 inch thick. Marinate in a combination of:

½ measure vinegar
½ measure water
1 Tbls. salt for every quart of water
8 bay leaves
8 whole cloves (optional)

uid. Rinse slightly with water and dry with a cloth. Best if fried in melted beef suet. Salt and pepper to taste. Sear both sides, then fry until done, turning frequently. Cook until medium well done. Brush with butter.

Mert's Jerky

Here's a good way to make use of your odd sized pieces and cuts that aren't too tender. Whatever meat you use, make certain to trim and remove all fat.

Cut venison in slices ¼ inch thick. With a meat hammer, pound both sides until uniform thickness. Seasonings consist of salt, pepper, onion powder, garlic powder, liquid smoke and water. Try a small batch first to season for taste. Combine seasoning. Spread meat in shallow pan and brush on seasonings. Pierce the end of each strip of venison with a round toothpick and hang in oven rack. Heat at low temp with oven door propped open slightly. Normal time is 18-24 hours.

HUNTER HINT

Keep on high ground as is consistent with quiet walking and wind direction.

Hunts from other times

Lystig Crew
Hillsdale/Dallas, WI.
1941-1950

Strangers wandered into camp
Cable Country - 1941

1948 - Winter, WI
Between the Mooses

Morris Lystig - 1946

Vern Holmen, Morris Lystig

Vern Holmen, Morris Lystig,
Milton Haugestuen

Irv Haugestuen &
Vern Holmen

"Here, you lift and I'll pull."

Curiosity killed cats even
back in the 40's

Irv Haugestuen - 1948

Irv Haugestuen,
Harold Engledew, Vern Holmen.

One thing about heating with wood.
It warms you up many times.

From the Morris Lystig
Hunting Album
Mid to Late 1940's
Chequamegon Forest
"Between the Mooses"
Winter, WI
Morris Lystig
Irv Haugestuen
Milton Haugestuen
Vernon Holmen
Harold Engledew

Eric Pagenkoph - Bloomer, WI
His first buck.

Lyell Cowley - Port Wing, WI
"A pioneer of Wisconsin Bowhunting."
1977 - His last buck.

Zesiger Deer Camp - Meteor, WI   1975.

Kenneth Lund
Buck shot near Chetek
Barron Co., WI

Kenny, Kenneth, Amy Lund
8 mi. East of Gordon, Douglas Co., WI

136

Kirk Haugestuen
Barron, WI.
"He's learned well."

Another dandy 18" spread.

Kirk's bow buck.

*Taken on successive days while sneak
hunting - Kirk prefers the solo hunt.*

The Lucas Gang
Solon Springs, WI.
1964-1967

Jackie Lucas   1967

Leo Lucas - 1967
Wt. 178#, 6 oz.
Horns weighed 12 pounds

Courtesy Bob Prevost - Prevost's Restaurant/Bar/Sportshop   Solon Springs, WI

The Lucas Gang

Reil Prevost and
some Lucas bucks.

*One must
remember:
"Believe none
of what
you hear . . .*

*. . . and
only half
of what
you see."*

Reil Prevost and his lunker muskie.
Is this some kind of a record?

Courtesy Bob Prevost - Prevost's Restaurant/Bar/Sportshop   Solon Springs, WI

139

Burnett Muermann
Barron Co.   1942-43

1947 - Muermann Camp
Iron River, WI.

Edward Jansen - 1940
10 point Buck - 23½ inside spread
Shot near the Barron/Polk Co. Line.

Walt Kittleson Camp   1931
Left to right: Eng Arneson, Walt Kittleson,
Carl Anderson, Elwood Johnson,
Harold Amundson

The Nehr-Bit Gang
Danbury, WI

*Waldron Bitney, Bill Nehring, Butch Nehring,
T-Bone Bitney, Howard Nehring, Eph Bitney*

*Eph Bitney's Bear and Max Stuckert.
Shot with a 33 Winchester.
1938   490#*

*T-Bone Bitney, Eph Bitney
Buckhorn Camp
1963*

*An Early Wisconsin Bowhunt
Necedah   1946
Top: Clarence Gorges, Eph Bitney,
Ray Mullen, Gib Sarazen, Doug
Weideman, Howard Nehring.
Bottom: Ollie Nehring, Verlyn Bitney,
Claude Klund, Gordy Barthen, Bill
Koepke, unknown hunter.*

*"The Camp Cook" Myrtle
Bitney, Eph Bitney, and Verlyn
Bitney seated.
Nehr-Bit Camp*

Zane Bitney - 1971
10 pointer north of the Nehr-Bit

Bernie Bitney
"The High Rack"

Nehr-Bit Lodge
1989
Left to Right: Verlyn Bitney,
Steven Scoll, Lee Jamison,
Chris Nehring, Bill Nehring,
Chip Dearing, Butch Nehring,
Bernie Bitney, Jeff Bitney.

Howard Nehring
1968

Butch Nehring

<u>Authors Note:</u>

The following pages are detailed accounts of actual hunts which took place in the early days of the Nehr-Bit Camp of Burnett County, Wisconsin. These entries into the Camp Log were originally hand written by Zane Bitney. The originals, however, suffered the ravages of time, so for both clarity and necessity to conserve space it was required they be rewritten. These copies are in exact duplication of the originals both in style and in content.

These are accounts of how deer hunting used to be, written by one who experienced the hunts.

Jan. 4, 48

The Big Hot 47 Hunt

By Z.C.B.

It was the day before opening day of rifle season & I was at the garage trying to keep my mind on my work. Dad & Howard had left early this day to set up camp & get thing cozy for a full week of nerve wracking excitement. After 3 hours of driving in semi-darkness of the early morn & a slight rain they reached their destination & proceeded to pitch the tent. (The spot they picked was by that gravel pit where you & dad caught the trought.)

After the tent was securely pegged to the ground so it couldn't blow away, they filled it up with provisions. First of all came the wood. They cut enough wood to last 2 weeks at the least. Then they made the bed, which consisted of pegs in the ground for corner posts, & then rails to hold the straw in. The straw was a foot deep covered with blankets & then sleeping bags. Then came the stove & they made a table & moved in the food & by the time this was completed they had the lanterns going full blast. Then they started to cook something to eat. Then the Editor (Tiy) & I came in & we ate a little bit and went to bed. All this while Verlyn is going to school & has to play basket ball that night, so he comes up with Clayton Boise at 1:30. After he crawls in & everything is quiet except for snores, grunts, & what have you when people are sleeping it rolls around to 5:00 & we get up & grab a few bites to eat & are on our way. Tip, Verlyn, & I go up to the field & go east on a fire lane. We leave Tip by the road cause he doesn't believe in a compass & I wasn't going to go around looking for him the first night. So after leaving Tip off Verlyn & I proceeded down the fire lane with the utmost precaution not to make noise. After going a half

144

a mile on tip toes we spy some jokers up ahead of us talking so we barged right on down & went to our stands. Verlyn stopped on a ~~×××~~ well packed run way on the fire lane & I went down to a cedar swamp & went along the bank to my stand that I had picked out. But on the way I spied a bucks track coming out of the swamp going west & I thought other hunters coming in would chase him back to me so I perched by a stump & stayed there.

In the meantime Dad & Howard went in East from camp on a fire lane & were walking along, and all of a sudden a big buck comes running along and stops a fair distance ahead of them so Dad whispers to Howard, "You shoot & I'll shoot at the same time." So they ~~jus~~ takes a deadly aim & Ba-loom a deafening roar of a 33 whinchester & a 32 special splits the still morning and 1 buck drops to the ground. They dash madly to the scene of slaughter & there he was both front legs broke. He was still very much alive yet so dad very nobly puts another piece of lead through his neck. The buck goes limp & they wait for him to die. Then it jumped up on its hind feet & makes a clumsy lunge in their direction. So being a very obliging fellow my father shoots him again through the neck. The buck goes limp. After a short while he comes to and makes another lunge. So dad's temper has a limit, same as any man, so he ups & ~~bla~~blasts him through the back of the head & does everything but blow his horns off & this time he's really dead. So Howard proceeds to drag the prize back to camp. It's already about 9:30 & I'm still at my stump. ~~So~~ Tip & Verlyn are at parts unknown so we'll get back to Dad. While Howard is dragging the Buck to Camp dad sneaks down a little farther & stands. About 5 minutes later a buck comes down the trail & dad ups & bang!! the buck stops, & dad keeps on shooting

(3)

bang!! bang!! bang!! the buck stands there + then dad sees white spots in front of the bucks shoulders + he thinks he can see holes right through the deer. So he goes to shoot again + click the guns empty so dad goes down on his knee + puts a shell in his gun ~~&~~ shoots again. (Correction on the first 2 shots, he hit the deer in the neck 2 times before he stops.) So after running out of shells he shoots 4 shots at him + he stands their + then he shoots one more shell + the buck goes down. So he goes up to the deer + can't find it. Then he looks around + finds the deer was farther away than he figgered so he goes on farther and their was the deer, deader than an old tin can. Then looking around he sees his fault for not killing the deer. The 4 shots after the deer stopped (3) had gone through an iron wood tree 3 inches thick + a popple tree 4 inches + then hit the deer, burn't the hair + fell off. The fourth shot just went through the popple + got into the deers hide but he never moved. He must have been dazed to much to run. Then the 5th shot he missed the tree + killed the deer. I'm still on my stump + Verlyn + Tip are in parts unknown. Howard comes back + he goes over to Dad + they decide to stand around awhile so Howard goes over the hill from Dad + Bang!!, Bang!!, Bang!!. + soon Howard comes over the hill practically on the run with a deer by the horns. So they had 3 deer + I'm still on my stump + Tip is in parts unknown. Verlyn is showing some joker how his gun comes apart + a buck goes tearing by + he slaps it back together + shoot 2 shots + missed. Then I started to wake up. I hears something over to my right ~~s~~ so ~~I~~ being kinda disgusted from standing their so long (5 hrs) + not seeing a thing except 4 does I just turned right around + here

Dad had his glasses on + the deer looked clear.

(4)

was a nice buck 40 ft. away looking right at me. I had my gun butt on the ground & my right had on the barrel & so I stood & looked right back at him. Finally what seemed like eternity he turned & walked behind a pine tree & nibbled on a little grass & then I went into action. I threw the gun up to my shoulder & followed him along & when he came out the other side I let drive. I knocked him through the front shoulders & he humped up & took off in a mighty leap & down into the swamp. I snapped another shot at him & he hit a tree & dug his horns in the snow & piled up. & so I had mine. The second shot missed. Good thing cause the first one was enough. I dragged him out & half way Verlyn caught up with me. I toll some fellas if they saw a kid with a vermein automatic to tell him to get to hell down the fire lane & help me. So we went to camp. Tip was there & all he had done was move around all morning & had seen nothing. Then some fellas from town came into camp & said dad & Howard had 2 more deer up the fire lane a ways so I went up their & helped drag them in. and that was the end of the day. The next day we seen nothing so Tip & I had to come home for work. & verlyn came back to school. Dad & Howard stayed up & tried to get one more to fill up so Tip would have one but didn't see a thing so came home. tues night. thats a detailed subscription of the hunt.

all he had was his handkerchief to dry with

Zane

147

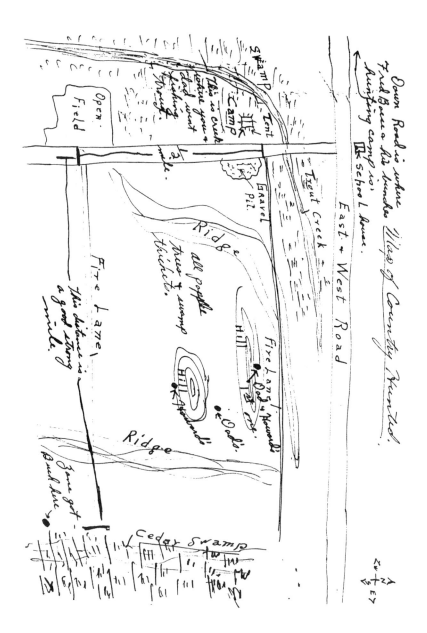

Jan 17, 1949

The Hunt
Nov. 48

As Narrated
By Zane
Bitney

The week before the hunting trip was a very long one. Getting everything lined up gave Father 10 extra gray hairs. Ma did that (he says he won't go hunting anymore. He does the worrying for the whole bunch). Finally Thursday finally rolled around & we were to leave Friday morning. We had sufficient snow for tracking so spirits were pretty high. Thursday night I stayed down to the garage & put on a trailer hitch. I had drills, hammers, cutting torches & arc welders all going at once. I had to use my feet once in awhile to keep them all going. Finally the great Nash was ready to roll. I went home & Dad & Howard had the trailer all packed & everything on the porch ready to go. I arrived at the Bitney residence at 9:00 & then the weather threatened to be nasty. It started to rain. This would make the roads slippery & very treacherous especially with a trailer on behind so we decided to leave right away. Arms legs and supplies were flying around like mad. We got the car loaded to the axles & trailer re-adjusted. Then a race up to Howards for bedding & more food, guns, & ammo. Then back to home for the hitch & take off. Then a disaster struck. I was dumbfounded!! All my mechanical genius & mathematical calculations were wrong! The trailer hitch wouldn't fit the hitch on the car. All this time its raining half snow & half rain. Then a mad dash up to the pea factory where Howard worked in the shop. A screetch of brakes & a flash of a cutting torch & metal being cut & then the Nash roared down the highway to home again. This time it fit. Now it is 9:50 + we wave goodbye to the folks at home + set out on our 112 mile trip to the north woods. It really nasty out now + its very hard driving. A strong north wind keeps me in direct drive cause I didn't dare go fast enough to get it in Overdrive and keep it there. I could only go 50 M.P.H. in direct. I must have gained on a few hills cause we made Spooner in an hour + 15 min. After we left Spooner the rain stopped + now it was snow. Not very heavy + it was cold so it wasn't slushy. I kicked it in overdrive, + rolled 55 + 60. New blacktop road smooth as glass. Soaring on H.70 over to H.35 was kinda slow, lots of curves + hills. When we hit H.35 it was straight + Not snowing now. I turned on the radio + got some western music from Cinn. Ohio. It came in nice + clear + the road was smooth. so we rolled 60-65. no wind bothering now cause trees on both sides stopped it. We couldn't even hear the motor it ran so quiet. It was just like flying with no motor. Finally we reached our destination. We got out the two gas lamps we had along + lit them. We cleared away the ground + set up the tent. then we were going to cook a lunch + everything was there except the frying pans. "Holy Balls" the old man said. "I bet they're still at home on the stove." He said, "I seen them setting there, but never put them in." I went out + looked the car over again + lo + behold, there they were in the trunk. "Good thing we got Momma," I said, "Or, we'd leave home + leave our ass sitting in a chair." She had put them in the trunk. We ate a lunch + went to bed. 4:30 in the morning and now its snowing like mad. Oh yes, we seen

2 deer on the way down the hill towards the creek
so felt pretty good. We are now sleeping. Snores,
whistles, grunts, & peculiar noises fill the air
surrounding the tent until 12 noon on Friday. Then
we wake up & eat & its still snowing. Dad, Howard,
and I leave for a short walk. To look for Camp Meat??
Could because I had a P38 in my pocket. We went
south on the road to the field + then cut west to the
ridge + follow it back to Camp. Seen lots of tracks
but no meat. Back at camp we secure the tent
a little bit better + go to sleep. Sat. morning up
bright and early + out for the kill. We decide that
Nadine should go up the hill + west to the ridge
+ hunt there cause there was some good runways there.
Dad + Howard go straight East of Camp like last year
+ I go to my old stand. I stay at my stand until
nearly noon then Dad + Howard come along + go south
farther into the swamp + I double back towards camp
+ go west across the field + over to the ridge + meet
Dad + we start towards camp. We get to camp and
Nadine has an 8 point buck already for us to hang
up. One big heart to save for a few more. We
talk over the hunt + come to find out Nadine had gone
on the ridge + heard some shooting further west so
goes down the fire lane to a little swamp + here
comes 2 bucks + a doe so she shoots the buck in the
rear cause the first one was quite a ways away.
She hits him in the ribs + he lays down + staggers a-
round + a little bit + an Indian Kid finishes it
off for her. She drags it down to the ridge + then she
starts down the ridge. Whoops!! careful. I knew it

she ships first she's riding the buck down the hill then shift the buck is riding her & finally after the toboggan party is over she stops at the bottom & continues dragging the buck to the creek. There she stops whew. Can't go any farther. she goes over to camp & leaves the buck lay but she can still see it so its safe. then she goes to unload her gun. Howards 33 lever action. One shell comes out & the second one goes **Bang** !!! down through the blankets Howards diddy bag & on into the ground. Guess she's kinda excited. Cy Schultz & Joe Paulus come along & drag her buck into camp & go on hunting. All this time We are out hunting & don't even see a horn. But we are pretty well satisfied anyway. It's very hard hunting cause the snow is hanging on the trees & its cloudy & misty out all the time & it cut visibility down to no good in the woods. We go to bed & next morning we go off again & I go to my stand only down the point where the swamp & the ridge come together. good spot. Dad goes east only a little ways & Nadine goes on the ridge. I get to my stand at 7:00 & get all set & I lean up against a tree & relax then I see a herd of deer 4 of them it's still dusk but can see the sights. they come out of the tagalders & then I see horns I raise my rifle & wait till he gets away from the does & then he stands still. Oh, boy broadside standing shot I take aim start squeezing the trigger & then he whirls & takes off into the tagalders. I snaps a quick shot at his shadow & then he disappears. ©#!©*M©¢ (cuss words) I missed him! I stand there & wait I'm just about ready to go down to see if I hit him &

then the 3 does come out & dash in a circle around me & then praise be the buck comes out & I snaps a shot at him & he keeps on going. He goes towards the swamp & will be out of sight soon so I take a bead on his shoulders & follows him along & then bang or it was more of a "Baloom" as my mighty 33 breaks the silence for the 3rd time & then the buck disappears & still don't know if I hit him or not. Then a guy comes out of the swamp right where the buck came from & hollers "did you get him" I said I didn't know. He said "What you mean you don't know" I figgered he'd made enough noise to scare all the deer out of the country so I go down to look. I sneaks over to where he disappeared ready to shoot if he gets up but he didn't. I hit him the 3rd shot & he slid to a scrunching halt right there. The first shot I broke his hind leg at the knee & the second shot I missed & the 3rd shot I hit him in the heart area. I cleaned him out & started dragging him to camp. Howard said if either one of us got one we should whistle a long & 2 short so I blew myself dizzy. But no Howard. So I start dragging + 8:30 & all along the fire lane I whistle & whistle But no answer. So I continue dragging then at 12:00 I finally crawl into camp. Dad comes in & Nadine is already there so we shoot the bull for awhile & then Howard comes in & we hang it up and we figger on 2 hearts for supper. When we reach up into the carcass for the heart & we get a handful of mush. I hit him in the heart. lucky shot. we go to bed. Next day Mon. We all hunted East of camp in the swamp & nothing happened until we ~~kicked~~ drove the swamp

& kicked a spike out onto Nadine & she shot it
& drew blood so we started tracking. I circled up on a
ridge & I seen a deer down below me & hollered to
dad & he walked over to them & I figgered it was
the buck & I started to go towards it cause dad was
nearly standing on it. When I started down up got
a big doe & 2 fawns. Howard thought it was the buck
& couldn't see to good & cut loose with the 8 mm.
bolt action. He missed & then his gun fell apart. The clip
fell out like it did on you. I found the bucks track &
we trailed it dad on my left & Howard on the right.
we tracked it back a good ½ mile & it was getting
dusk & I speeded up a little Bit & kept looking ahead
then I seen it. about like the house to the woodshed.
He was laying down & looking straight ahead away from
me so I up & shot him in the back of the head &
he relaxed. When we got to it, it was just an illegal
spike. We cleaned it out & dragged it back to camp
& hid it. Then we went to camp & went to bed = the
next day. Tue Nothing Tue Hunted like mad & no deer.
Wed. Nothing all day except dad seen a big deer
way across a ravine so he up & shoots hoping its
a buck. & first shot it goes down then after a little
wait it gets up & he shoots again it goes down. He
waits awhile & goes over there & he has a young buck
& a doe piled up about 15 ft. apart. Good shooting.
Wed. night we put the deer "spike" in the trunk & then
we hunt till noon & nothing around so come home.

The End

Yours truly
Zane Pitney

"Dad said he felt so bad about
his game & he had seen anyone pull
a stunt like that he would have kicked
their ass clear out of the woods."

"The 49 Hunt"

By Zane Bitney

It seems that every year about the middle of November, that everybody & his brother wants to go hunting. Being that the deer season is open around this time, they all go deer hunting. Usually the season is open only for a buck having a forked horn with a fork no less than 1 inch. This year the Conservation Dept. got a bug & said they would have an antlerless deer season. This included Does, fawns, spike bucks & bucks having a forked horn, but the fork could not exceed 2 inches. Therefore - all the hunters carried a 2 inch measuring stick with them so if they seen a buck with a forked horn going through the thick swamp, they could run up alongside of him, measure his horn & if it was legal they could stop take aim & "BOOM!!" either miss or kill their deer. So under these conditions we proceeded to get prepared for the opening day of the season. As usual Dad had most everything ready a week ahead of time & the trailer all set to be loaded. Because I run in a cycle I didn't put my trailer hitch on until the night before, same as usual. We Dad & I & "Dale" planned to go up Fri. noon & pitch camp. We loaded up and down the road we went. We didn't have any snow as yet but were supposed to get snow that night so we had our hopes pretty high. Nadine couldn't go the last thing because she got a blood clot in her leg & was put in the hospital. Howard & Ralph Breunig were coming up at night after (Ralph) Toozy finished work. He always wanted to go with us but could never get off, but this year he got a chance so he came along. We arrived at our campsite at 3:30 & started to put up the tent. Our table & bed frame was still there & most of the stakes to. We put the tent up, staked it down, set up our stove, made the bed & we were all set. We took our little box heater for heat + we had a little 2 burner shelgas stove for cooking. We made a little supper + went to bed. About 3:00 Howard + Foozy got there. Slight interruptions in our slumber + then all was quiet. The next morning at 6:00 we were up + eating breakfast. Dad, Howard, + Dale were going west of camp on the ridge this time + Foozy + I went way back where I got my deer last year. Foozy + I took the car up to the field + then walked back in on the logging road to our stands. We no sooner got standing when all Hell broke loose. It seemed like everyone else was shooting except Foozy + I. After standing 2 hrs. I was rewarded by a glimpse of a doe way down in the swamp about 400 yds. away. All I could see was her head sticking around a tree looking straight at me. I took aim + "BOOM" - "Wacho" I hit a tree between here + there. She stands + looks at me. 4 more times I shoot + 4 more times I hit trees so I gave up. We looked at one another for awhile + finally she wiggles her ears, turns around wiggles her tail + off she goes. I walked down to the spot + on the way down I could see spots on the tree where I was hitting. I stood down there awhile + then I got to thinking my sights may have gotten banged up so I was going to take a practice shot. When I tried the gun out I hit a 6 inch bullseye at 45 yards. I seen a snowshoe rabbit about 30 yds. away so I up + "BOOM!!" the rabbit dissolves + there is nothing left but a little hair. I knew then the gun was all right. I went back to my stand + nothing was moving. Foozy came down + stood with me awhile he hadn't seen a darn thing. It was snowing a little now + the ground was turning a little white. The snow was wet + it hung to the trees, same as last year, but not quite so bad. We decided to go back towards camp so we goes up along the swamp over the big ridge + up to the East + West swamp that goes down to camp. I put Foozy on top of the ridge bordering the swamp on the South + told him to follow that + he'd come out at camp + I would take the swamp. He didn't have a compass but I didn't think he'd go off the ridge so never thought to give him mine.

I goes down through the swamp & finally reaches camp. No Foozy! Dad was there & Howard & Dale. Dad had shot a fawn for Dale & Howard had one back in the woods hid. I ate a little lunch & was just going to start tracking foozy down when into camp he came all pooped out. He went off the ridge, worked south, then southeast, then east & was headed for the river when he ran into a man & got his directions. This other fellow was headed out so Foozy went out with him. He was really tired so he stayed in camp in the afternoon. He was wet clear through so he had to dry out.

Dad, Howard, & I went west of camp in the afternoon & we no sooner reached the top of the ridge when we jumped one & Howard shot 4 times but didn't hit so we went down the ridge & scattered out & stood. Nothing happened until "Bloom" "Bloom" 2 shots broke the still afternoon & it was Dad. He got a nice spike buck with spikes about 4 inches long. We went up & started to drag it back to camp. Dale & Foozy were in camp yet. Dale couldn't hunt anymore because he had his deer. After a man got his deer he wasn't allowed to carry a gun any more. When we got up on the ridge straight west of Camp Howard Decided to go back & get the one he shot. He was turned around all morning himself so he didn't know quite where his deer was but we figured out pretty close & went after it. We finally found it & we got back to camp just at dusk so we ate supper & went to bed. Foozy put his tag on the one Howard shot. The next morning Howard & I went back west again & I stood where Dad got his spike & Howard stood on the bank by the ridge. On the way in there we kicked out 3, 2 does & 1 buck, the buck was illegal & we didn't get a chance at the Does so we stood. Finally Dad & Foozy came through on a little drive but never chased anything out. They weren't allowed to carry guns so they carried sticks & made a lot of noise. Then we went way back in west & Dad & Foozy went through a swamp on a little drive but nothing came out. Foozy got a wet foot so he came back to me & said Dad & Howard were going to way back west & asked him if he was supposed to stay there or not & he said not so I went back with him to make sure he would get out OK. & then I went back on the stand where dad got his deer. When I got there, there were 3 deer had passed within 10 feet of the stand so I decided to stay there. About 11 'oclock a horn started to blow & it sounded like mine & then I wasn't sure so I stood there somemore then finally I decided to go to camp & see. I got up on the ridge & there were cars & people at camp & I thought something was wrong so I tore down the ridge about 40 per & when I got to camp Dad was there & said Howard had 2 deer back in the woods so I left my gun at camp & we went back. We took Mutts bunch back with us & put them on a drive & when we got to Howard they started their drive. We had a lunch for Howard & he was eating that & those other fellows were just out of sight & 3 shots rang out & then 1 more & we heard a deer blat so we knew they got one for sure. Dad picked up Howard's gun (the only one we had) & watched. He gave it to me & said I could probably hit more. So we waited. Whup here comes a nice big doe. About 300 yards away, I was going to shoot but then she was coming in our direction so I waited. She came closer & closer until she was broadside about 50 ft. so I let drive & took the heart out of her & we had 3 deer & only 2 tags so I took the Doe & we took the fawn that was mine & hid it. Then we started out. Mutt came over there so we told him where the fawn was & he went back & got it. We started back to camp & on the way we seen 7 deer. Howard & Mutt shot at them but they were quite aways away + didn't hit. We went into camp & tore it down + came home. We left there at 3:30 + got home at 7:00. It snowed all day Sat. + it was 2 or 3 inches deep + Sun. it was a little colder but just right. The roads were icy on the way home so could only go 35 so it took quite a while. Fred Boese's bunch filled up (10) the first day, Howie Koehler + all that bunch filled up & Mutts bunch filled up so there were quite a few deer taken out.

The End

Zane Bitney

THE HUNT

(As told to Chief Shoot-Um Heart Out by Chief Old Buck Killer)

Dawn on Wednesday, 16 Nov. 1955, found a raging blizzard piling snow upon the landscape to depths up to three and four feet. The entire length of Wisconsin felt the wrath of the storm and in the north woods the wind and snow howled over the birch ridges and was quieted to slowly sifting white in the pines. At the height of the storm visibility was reduced to a few yards and only the most hardy of man and beast ventured forth. This was the situation I faced when I headed north from Illinois on Thursday morning to prepare for the great slaughter that was to take place in the next few days.

The trip north was uneventful, leaving at 0730 and arriving in Bloomer at 1930 the same day. I had icy roads from the Dells to Black River Falls but from there on had clear sailing. Howard, Dad and Dale had the trailer just about all packed when I arrived and Ma had all the grub ready to be loaded in the morning. Friday morning, Howard, Nadine and four kids and Dale finished loading the trailer and headed for camp. Dad, ma and I came up later. Had to get my license and other odds and ends plus see Helen and kids off for her mothers. We left about 0900 and had good roads to Spooner and ice on 70 and 35. Got to camp with no trouble and helped get everything set up. Banked the cabin with snow and after one trip to the one-holer Dad banked that too.

About 1400 we were all set up so went out to look over out stands for the next and opening day. Howard, Nadine and Dale went in on the pulp road off the east-west road, cross the creek into birch ridges past Howard's stand and where the beer cans are, then west into the oak ridges (where you gut shot one), then south up Perkins creek and climbed the high ridge into the field with their tails dragging in the snow. Dad and I went in east from the gravel pit along the high ridge along the creek back to your stand, then south through birch ridges and out to bottom of field hill. Dad was breaking trail at first but the snow was so deep or else his legs so short that his butt leveled his trail. The snow was a good foot deep and in swamps and in deep grass it was deeper. Due to the new snow there were very few tracks and hard to figure the best place to stand. By relying on the old woodsman and hunter instinct we selected our sites. I was going to stand on ridge along swamp east of where Dad got his second buck last year. Dad was going to stand a little further east and north along same swamp. With these decisions made, we returned to camp in the waning daylight to partake of a hearty meal and a final check of our gear before venturing forth opening morning. Howard, Nadine and Dale went in on the pulp road and set up their stands.

Saturday 1st day of Hunt

Lights were turned on at 0500 in response to the alarm ringing but I think everyone had been awake at least 15 minutes prior to 0500 waiting for the clock to ring. Howard made breakfast as he did each morning, and the rest of us made our final checks of our gear and lunches. Breakfast hurriedly eaten we took to our respective stands in the woods just before daybreak to be sure not to waste a minute of the hunting time allowed. I had 3 birch trees to lean on and cleaned all the snow from under foot so as not to slip in case of fast shooting. Dad went over to his stand and almost immediately spotted the hind quarters of a deer in the buck brush. He tried to see the head or horns but could not make them out in the faint morning light. He watched the deer for about 5 or 10 minutes and never did see it's head so assumed it was a doe the way it acted. It wandered off and Dad didn't shoot. Later I came over to his stand and he went down to look at the track and here it had been a big buck. I went down the trail we had made the day before and dad took the track. I picked out a good stand and here came Dad right up to me following the track. The deer had passed prior to my arrival. All this happened about 1100 and we still hunted along over to your stand. Mutt and Bill Dierk were standing there talking. A big buck had his bed right on top of your stand waiting for you and when Mutt came along he took off and Mutt missed him. Worked our way north and west the rest of the day but didn't see anything. Stood on the creek bank for a while but saw nothing. Howard and others saw some does but no shooting. Weather was cloudy at about 25 degrees. Returned to camp all pooped and a little discouraged to think that no one had even seen one let alone shoot one. However everyone went to bed early with blood in their eye and a do or die attitude for the next day. Score: 4-0 favor of the deer.

Sunday 2nd day of the Hunt

Teamed up with Mutt, Bill and Art Dierk and Gregg Goettel to drive the corner formed by the north-south east-west road and the pulp road. Started the drive from the swamp east of the pulp road and drove thru to the roads. Bill Dierk, who was driving next to me, got a snap shot at a big buck but hit a big tree-Timberrrrrr. I went over on the creek bank east of the gravel pit and then worked my way around the trail. Was on your stand when Dad came through. He had kicked out 4 deer in one pot hole and took a couple of half-hearted shots which missed. All does anyway. Nadine went home with Dads car and we used Howards after that. I followed our trail on around and came out by the field seeing nothing. Howard picked up a buck track west of the field, crossed the road down where Norby emptied his gun in the brush, went right past my stump down on the big swamp and into the river. Weather was about 35 degrees and I was wet from my waist down. No deer and things looked a little rough. Two day gone by and no deer and Stuckards had five hung up. Score: 4-0 favor of the deer.

Monday 3rd day of the Hunt

Monday dawned dark, cloudy and snowing up a storm. Temperature about 30 degrees with a little wind out of the NW. Dad and I went down by the big swamp and I got on my stump and Dad went on down to the point. Howard and Dale came in from the road but nothing happened. Howard and I went across the swamp and drove north thru the pines up to the road and Dad and Dale were on stands. Still nothing. Dale and Howard went north and drove along the river south. I was standing under a couple pine trees in a little swamp trying to see thru the snow. Dad was more out in the open and closer to the river. After standing there for what seemed all day, I saw two shadows sneaking thru the swamp about sixty yards in front of me. I couldn't see their heads let alone horns, it was snowing too hard so I figured the first one was a doe and the second a buck. I let the first one go by a little opening and took aim on the second and followed him to this little opening. The doe may have seen this movement and she stopped so the buck stopped also. His mistake was that he stopped right in my little opening and evidently turned his head and looked at me. That was his fatal mistake as I took careful aim and slowly squeezed the trigger. The quiet of the forest was suddenly broken by the roar of a pent-up .348. Birds twittered nervously and the snow seemed to pause temporarily in it's downward flight. All was quiet again except for the roar of the rapids in the river. The deer looked like it fell over backward and disappeared. I saw the does flag and that was all. I waited for Howard and Dale to finish the drive and then Dad came over and we went to look for the deer. He had make just one jump and that was all. As we neared him all we could see was one horn and that was a straight spike but the other had a "Y" that was just legal. There were three bullet holes in his neck which cut his throat and one came out his right front shoulder. I am at a loss to explain those three neck wounds, unless he had it twisted looking towards me. He melted a four inch diameter hole in the snow where he bled to death. Dressed him out and dragged him up to the logging road and loaded him on the car and back to camp to hang him up. We saw a fresh buck track where the logging road joins the main road so hurried back and Howard, Dale and Dad strung out along the road up to the hill and I took the track. He angled west and south and then headed straight west. I made a circle and came out about where the buck Norby shot at, but nothing happened. We went back to camp feeling considerably better and with hopes of continued success. Score: 3-1 favor of the deer.

Tuesday 4th day of the Hunt

Sky was cloudy but temperature was up around 35 degrees - typical wet clean to your a-- kind of weather. Teamed up with Mutt's bunch and went back down and drove the river again, but no luck this time. Howard took a fresh track headed south so Dad, Dale and I took our stands from the stump on the swamp south and waited. Howard ran the buck onto someone else and it sounded like a small arms war. Howard and Dad went out to the road and Dale and I drove through. I hit a blood trail about half way through so I followed that out to the logging road. Went back in to finish drive out to Howard and I heard him shoot three times so figured he either had one or a fresher blood track to follow. Howard was standing on the hill south of the field and one had sneaked up behind him. He had three shots on the fly but no hair or blood. We

were going to trail him but heard some other shooting so fig-
ured someone else would be on his trail. There was a trailer
with four men just beyond the hill which was all the hunters
in the entire area. Mutt's crew went home Tues. morning so
we had entire area to ourselves. Stuckards were hunting over
on the highway so we had no competition or anyone to move
the deer. Howard, Dale and I went back and took the blood
track I had followed and it petered out and we lost it in a little
ways. Howard took another track so I went over on the creek
bank and waited but he made a tight circle and came out where
Dad shot his second buck last year. Dad was sneak hunting
back in by your stand when he jumped one so took the track.
He sneaked over a hill and was trying to spot him in the buck
brush when out he went and ran up on the far side hill and
stopped. Dad knew he was a buck from his track, so took a
rest on a tree and blazed away. Deer jumped straight up in the
air and disappeared. Dad stood and waited 30 minutes keep-
ing his eye peeled for more before he started over to see the
results. Got over to where the deer was suppose to be and no
deer, track or anything. Dad went back to where he was stand-
ing and decided he had looked on the wrong hillside. Went
out again and still couldn't find deer or track. Things started
to get a little nervous about that time, but suddenly he saw a
lot of red snow on the hill side. Went over and the deer had
made about three jumps, spraying both sides of his track with
blood, hooked his horn around a tree and there he lay. Was a
nice "Y" buck shot through the shoulders and just nicked the
heart. Distance on the shot was close to 400 yards. Dragged
him out and back to camp to hang up beside the first one.
Spirits were really soaring now and felt maybe we could fill
up. Needless to say I was wet, even my shorts. Score: 2-2.

Wednesday 5th day of the Hunt

Temperature about 15 with a 20 MPH wind from the west. Went over and drove that corner by the pulp road again only this time Dad and I came in from the road and Dale stood where we always parked the car in there and Howard in where he could watch the open swamp to the east. Didn't see or hear anything so when we were walking up to pulp road, to the car, here was the buck track big as a cow walking up the road. We had kicked it out and it hit the road between Howard and Dale and went into the swamp on the other side. He walked within 30 yards of the car but Dale must have been looking the other way. Went in east of the gravel pit then and made a drive out to the foot of the hill but not a thing. Went back to the pulp road and Howard took the track and Dad and I went in on fire lane across from Bleeces. We jumped a couple back in there and sneaked along trying to spot them again. Howard had got back on the birch ridge and he got a couple shots thru the brush at them, but too far away. Dad and I took stands along the creek and Howard and Dale made a little swing toward us. I was standing on a big stump looking around when I spotted this doe coming toward me. I followed her with the gun and kept looking behind her for a buck, but as my doe got closer I could see she had one horn. He stopped behind a tree about 15 yards from me and I thought he was a spike buck, so I wasn't going to shoot. He jumped out from behind the tree, stopped and turned his head and looked right at me as if to say, "I have a little point on this spike and am legal as hell". At this moment I decided he was too but my gun was pointed at his tail, so I slowly moved it up to his shoulder and let him have it. He pitched forward on his head and then staggered about forty yards over a little rise and disappeared. I got my glove tangled up in the trigger so couldn't get off another shot - not that I needed it. Waited until the rest came over and took his track. Blood on both sides of the trail as far as he went, which wasn't far. Shot him thru the shoulders and when we went to take his heart out all that was left was a handful of mush and the three corners. Dragged him out and back to camp with visions of probably filling up the next day. Score 3-1 our favor.

Thursday 6th day of the Hunt

Snowed about half and inch during the night and then turned off cold. Temperature around 0 degrees, clear and no wind. Went over and drove the corner again but didn't even see a fresh track. Made the same drive where I got the one yesterday - nothing. Drove the creek west of the gravel pit and then the swamp where I got my first one - nothing. Still hunted out to road - nothing, not even a fresh track. Kind of confusing as to where all the deer had gone to. Dad and rest went over to Stuckards and all they had was the 5 they got the first two days. Seems they were all split up hunting singly and in pairs so weren't doing any good. Mutt and his bunch were skunked. Score: 3-1 our favor.

Friday 7th day of the Hunt

Temperature was about 15 degrees with very little wind. We drove the creek west of the gravel pit with no luck so drove the corner again. Howard and I stood on the high ridge, Dad on the pulp road by the swamp and Dale made the drive. I didn't see or hear anything for a long time when all of a sudden it sounded like a small arms war over by the swamp. Six shots rang out loud and clear. Suddenly 2 more were fired followed very closely by one more and then silence. I figured someone must be target shooting over by the swamp. Either that or else Dad had piled up an entire herd. Dale came thru so I worked my way over where Dad was and here he had piled the big buck up. Saw him sneaking thru the swamp in the tall grass so his first shot broke a front leg, thru the brisket and stuck in the other leg (lead enclosed). He kept moving north thru the swamp and Dad followed him on the pulp road pouring it to him. He gut shot him and again thru the brisket. Finally, emptied his gun and deer still going. So here is Dad running down the pulp road with one eye on the deer, one eye on the road and with a very shaky right had trying to reload his gun. I imagine things really were excited for a few minutes. Took him the length of a block to load his gun and he blasted two more shots which evidently missed. Deer started straight away from him so he shot him in the tail and down he went for the last time. He was a big, old, rangy pile of skin and bones, at least 10 years older than God and only six teeth, one of which Dale picked out with his finger. He might make sausage or hamburger, but I'll bet you couldn't get a fork in the gravy. We dragged him out and back to camp; loaded up and was home by 1500. We skinned out the second one I shot and took him down to Reetzes and they cut him up. Have had a couple messes off him and he was real tender.

Came home (Ill) Sunday with little slippery road from Madison to Rockford, but no other trouble. Furnace was out when I got home and had to take the pipes down and clean them out before the fire would burn. Back on the job and all rested up and ready to go again.

Waldron

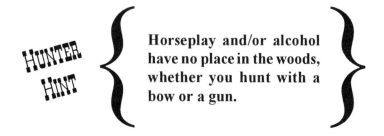

HUNTER HINT

Horseplay and/or alcohol have no place in the woods, whether you hunt with a bow or a gun.

Huntless Hunter

by Holly Meier

From the Chippewa Herald Telegram. Written by Holly Meier. The 1950 deer hunt of Ralph Breunig.

Weather conditions look promising as Wisconsin's deer hunters prepare for the state's nine-day season opening tomorrow (Saturday,) but Ralph Breunig, Chippewa Falls, couldn't care less.

I talked to Ralph Thursday morning at his desk in the First National Bank, and he allowed that while he was going deer hunting, he wasn't going to hunt.

"I think I'll just sit around the camp and drink coffee," he said, "but if a deer should wander up to the back steps, I might shoot it."

This reluctance to get into the woods was more understandable as Foozy (that's Ralph in Bloomerese) told of his baptism in the deer woods.

"I went up into camp with the Bitneys," he explained. "You know Eph Bitney, didn't you? Well, it must have been sometime shortly after midnight on a cold, bitter November morning when they rousted me out of bed, shoved a cup of coffee into my hand and a couple of sandwiches into my pocket, and led me out into the blackness."

"After stumbling around behind them for maybe an hour, we came to a stump," Fooz lamented, "and Eph put me on top of it."

"Sit there," Eph told Fooz, "and don't go stumbling around in the woods or you'll get lost. And don't," he warned, "go lighting any fires or you'll scare all the deer away. We'll come after you when it's time to go back to camp."

FOOZY SAYS HE "sat, and sat and sat," until finally grey dawn broke. "All I could see was trees and brush." he remembers. "There wasn't any snow, so I couldn't follow our tracks back to camp, and I didn't have the slightest idea where it was."

"By 9 in the morning my sandwiches were gone, and by noon I was so hungry I could have eaten the bark off the trees. I was cold and tired," Foozy recalls, "but afraid to leave the stump."

"By the time the Bitneys picked me up a 4:30 that afternoon I had packed down every blade of grass within a fifty-foot radius of that stump, walking around, trying to keep warm."

"I've gone deer hunting lots of times since that day," Breunig tells, "but I've never gotten out of sight of the camp."

The Chippewa Herald Telegram

The response to the article by Eph Bitney

REMEMBER THE story about Ralph "Foozy" Breunig going hunting with the Eph Bitney gang of Bloomer?

Eph writes:

"I am writing this to confirm the article written about my old hunting pal Foozie Breunig. Most of his story was true especially his six sandwiches, two candy bars plus the two apples that were gone by nine a.m.

"The ground around that stump was packed so hard that nothing has grown there since.

"Foozy didn't mention the nice warm sleeping bag that he tried to crawl into at night. I remember it took two of us to get him into it, and four to get him out of it the next morning.

"This was the year we were allowed to shoot only does, fawns, and spike bucks, protecting the fork horned bucks.

"Foozy and I got our deer the first morning, so all we could do after that was carry clubs. I remember Foozy saying if he met up with a bear he would feel safer with a club.

"Foozy and Zane Bitney built a pole bridge across a creek and that was when Foozy lost his watch which he never found. Every hunting season since that when we cross that pole bridge, I swear I can hear that watch ticking

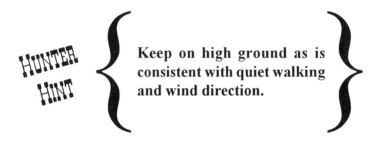

HUNTER HINT { Keep on high ground as is consistent with quiet walking and wind direction. }

If you appreciate fine sets of deer horns, it will be well worth your time to stop in at Poor Richard Antiques in Spooner, WI. Richard is a collector and owns many sets of large, heavy, and unusual typical and non-typical horns.

Richard show two sets of horns here with over a 27" spread. In his left hand is a single shed with a circumference of 10 inches. The world's record is reportedly 9 inches.

Note the drop tines on the large nontypical and the book head in his left hand

HUNTER HINT { **Keep on high ground as is consistent with quiet walking and wind direction.** }

They Border on the Prepostorous

Just Keeping Up©

1990   Mert Cowley

Harvey'd had some time to think
    on his drive home from the shack
"Another lousy year again
    I'm never going back
With all the second-hand old junk
    I have to use each year
Most other guys have what they need
    and hunt with decent gear."

Thoughts he had of this year's hunt
    were still fresh on his mind
"It took me longer fixing things
    than I spent for hunting time."
Just then his station wagon
    which had seen its better years
Began to lurch and sputter
    and started grinding gears.

"Oh, go ahead and quit again
    you rusty mangled heap
The day that I scratch up some cash
    You're the <u>last</u> thing that I'll keep
You and that beat up gun of mine
    I've had for umpteen years
It jams each time I need it
    and its cost me several deer."

The station wagon coughed again
    then seemed to come alive
Harv breathed a sigh of deep relief
    as he pulled into his drive
Just in time to see his neighbor
    Jones, returning home
His great big shiny pickup truck
    just glittering with chrome.

"Hey Harv, come here and take a look
    at what we've got in back
Three eights, a ten, and Mossy Horns
    with perfect twelve point rack
We drove back in, way off the road
    where hunters weren't so thick
It's great to own four wheel drive
    they really work out slick."

If ever there were words that may have
    broke the camel's back
The neighbor Jones braggin'
    was enough to make Harv crack
"That does it," thought poor Harvey
    as he turned a jealous green
"Next year I'll own the finest truck
    Old Jonesy's ever seen."

"I'm going to have to sacrifice
a whole year of my life
I'll dedicate my time to work,
despite the little wife
The extra money that I earn
I'll use to buy new gear
Next fall I'll have the things I need
to hunt the white tail deer."

On Monday morning Harvey stepped
up to the boss's desk
Said, "Sir, I have to bother you
I have a strange request.
Take my vacation time away
I'll work on holidays
Please put me down for overtime,
I'll take what jobs you say."

Harvey never knew exactly
when he'd eat or sleep
The double shifts he worked now
had him napping on his feet
But when the day his paycheck came
four figures made him smile
"At this rate I'll start buying things
in just a little while."

Within nine months Harv's bank account
huge figures had it grown
The banker <u>and</u> his brother-in-law
had asked him for a loan
At work he hummed his favorite tune,
over and over again
"A couple more hours of overtime,
Oh my, how the money rolls in."

One day he took an hour off
    and to the dealer went
and ordered out his custom truck
    complete with power vent
Extended cab with factory top
    and oversized snow tires
with winches mounted fore and aft
    In case he should get mired.

The clerk then at the rifle shop
    said, "Yes, what will it be?"
Harv settled for a magnum type
    hand made by Weatherby
"And mount a scope, a Leupold
    on second thought, a Zeiss
This makes a dandy combo and
    besides they <u>feel</u> so nice."

Harvey took his extra cash
    went North and bought some land
Four private wooded sections
    on which he placed his stand
He hired then a crew to build
    a hunting lodge of log
with fireplace and sauna
    and a kennel for his dog.

The day that Harvey's truck arrived
    he wore a constant grin
He drove it slow past Jones's house
    to sorta rub it in
He'd slip it into neutral
    and would rev it up real nice
Made Jonesy do a double take
    not once, but even twice.

Harvey asked for two weeks off
    with season drawing near
The first days Harvey hadn't worked
    for nearly now a year
He loaded up his brand new stuff
    into his brand new truck
To spend some time relaxing
    and this season, get his buck.

But on the morn of opener
    Poor Harv was sitting there
Perhaps in shock, in silence
    with an empty vacant stare
He shook his head and muttered then
    "It didn't help a bit
For all these things I had to have
    no license did I get."

The Winch©

1992   Mert Cowley

Barney'd put in overtime
    as he'd tried in vain to sleep
By counting monstrous whitetails
    as they'd jump through snowdrifts deep.
"I must come up with something
    once my buck is in the bag
To get it pulled back to my truck,
    without some three-hour drag."

His shout of, "Yes, I <u>have</u> it,"
    nearly scared his wife to death.
"My invention, when constructed
    will rank up there with the best
This thing which I have thought of
    will make dragging deer a cinch.
I'll mass produce and sell it as
    The Hunters' Pocket Winch."

He grabbed a pad and pencil
    as the thoughts raced through his mind
And listed things he'd have to make
    or borrow, buy, or find.
"I must have gears with perfect mesh,
    and cables from a plane
A 9 volt cell with cadmium
    rechargeable when drained.
A strap or chain to hook the winch
    onto a tree some way
Remote control, to turn it on
    from several yards away."

He built the winch with plastic case
    quite durable when cold
So compact in its size a man
    in one hand he could hold.
T'was small enough to carry
    on a belt or in a sack
Barney found it fit just right
    in his blaze orange fanny pack.

Barney on his stump did drop
    his buck just after dawn
And with it tagged, he put the winch
    to work before too long.
He snapped one cable to his buck
    the other to a tree
Stepped back, then touched remote control
    it worked right to a tee.

The second that he pushed the switch
    Things started working right
The tiny gears began to turn
    and drew the cable tight.
The buck began to slide along
    right up the gentle slope
The winch was working better
    than old Barney'd ever hoped.

It pulled the buck with utmost ease
    through swamp and over knob
The winch with gears reduction
    did perform a yeoman's job.
The only work that Barney did
    while dragging out his deer
Was now and then, rehook the winch
    hit the switch, and then stand clear.

Things went along so smoothly
    before long the drag would end
He'd have the deer right to his truck
    Then show it to his friends.
'This one's a trophy," Barney thought,
    "My finest buck of all.
I'll have a head mount made of it,
    and hang it on the wall."

Now somewhat bored and tired with
    but one short drag to do
Old Barney rested by his truck
    until the drag was through.
The bright warm sun upon his eyes
    their lids began to close
And Barney's head, began to nod,
    and he then began to doze.

The sound of leaves that rustled
    grinding gravel on the road
Brought Barney back from slumberland
    The winch had pulled its load.
He rubbed his eyes and there beside him
    lay his trophy buck
And Barney said, "In all my years,
    I've never had such luck.

Then Barney did a double-take
    for something wasn't right
Ye Gods! There lay the head and horns
    but no body was in sight.
From right behind the ears, its neck
    Looked like some sort of rope
Which wound its way across the ditch
    Then somewhere down the slope.

In panic Barney took off
    running faster than he should
Jumping stumps and deadfalls
    as he raced down through the woods.
The narrow neck he followed
    was a trail few will see
It led him to the body
    Which was wedged between the trees.

He had to pry, he tugged and tried
    Then finally had it loose
And dragged his prize up to his truck
    The winch, no longer used
To make it fit, he took the neck
    and looped it again and again
By the time the head was on the pile,
    rigormortis had set in.

In camp there was no sympathy
    or pity to be found
Instead were all his campmates
    in hysterics on the ground.
Some wise guy'd made the comment
    "When we hang <u>this</u> on the pole
We'll have to all get shovels
    and dig a deep, deep hole."

Ralph barely got the words out
    as the tears welled in his eyes
"We've got ourselves a <u>Guiness</u> here"
    as he viewed poor Barney's prize.
"Its head and horns, they won't make book
    it's the <u>neck length</u> if you please
That buck, no doubt, could peer around
    a record number of trees."

Then Weak Eyes had to chime in with,
    "I saw one like that, too.
I viewed the creature many times
    when I was at the zoo.
There was one difference in it, though,"
    and then he had to laugh.
"They didn't call the thing a deer,
    the sign, it said, 'Giraffe.' "

Barney said he'd heard enough
    and to his truck he ran
And drove to town to leave his buck
    with the taxidermy man
Who said, "This job will cost a lot
    I must think, "How in the heck?
Do I build up a form, and then make the mount
    of a deer with a forty foot neck?"

A year passed by, the call then came
    "Good news, your mount is done.
It took less time than figured
    and the work was kinda fun.
The cost I kept to a minimum
    I had just what it'd take.
I found out back, beneath some junk
    body forms for a King Cobra snake."

183

Barney said, "I like it!
It's like none I've seen before."
And placed it in his den at home
so it stares right at the door
His wife no longer cleans there
for when she turns on the light
She's face to face with an eight point buck
that's coiled, and ready to strike.

HUNTER HINT { Avoid going down wind. }

The Air Boots©

1992   Mert Cowley

His wife had Barney shopping there
    on Sunday at the mall
Not where he liked to find himself
    those early days of fall
It seems the little woman
    laid the rules out pretty clear
If Barney'd had his druthers
    he'd be up North scouting deer.

So Barney strolled around the mall
    twas cheap to window shop
He had to waste some time somehow
    his wife could go nonstop
He had some holdout money
    in the cabin fund this year
But it wasn't nearly what it'd take
    to head North hunting deer

The window of the sport shop
    showed some blaze orange hunting gear
He thought, "I'll have to use my
    faded stuff another year"
On down the hall he stopped to view
    some new athletic socks
And other things like sweatshirts
    which were just designed for jocks.

Then something caught his eye that was
    the latest fashion craze
Much different than the tennis shoes
    he'd worn in younger days
These shoes were fancy colored
    and what really had him stumped
It looked to be, built in the tongue
    some sort of tiny pump

He thought then of his hunting boots
    with soles wore paper thin
A tear across their rubber tops
    where water just poured in
The eyelets for the laces, either
    lost or terribly bent
The tongue the dog had chewed on
    which provided fresh air vents.

The brains of an inventor
    started putting things together
"There _is_ a way, to make some cash
    improve my life style better!
If I combine the comforts of a
    hunting boot with air
I'll sell a million of them
    at two hundred bucks a pair."

When he got home he headed for
    his workshop in the shed
And drew up plans straight through the night
    and never went to bed
He called in sick on Monday
    and said, "Get a substitute"
By noon had drawn the plans up for
    "Air Barneys Hunting Boot."

The list of items needed
    it was costly and quite long
But Barney knew by scrounging
    he could get things for a song
He'd always found the junkyard
    could supply his every need
And went to look, among the wrecks
    and searched with utmost speed.

For soles he took the recaps from
    a sideswiped Diamond T
And grabbed a stack of innertubes
    he knew he'd get for free
But soft and supple uppers
    had him stymied up until
He cut the leather seats out of
    a Caddy Coupe de Ville.

He knew that he'd be running tests
    on several kinds of liners
To see which kind performed the best
    Then use which was the finer
The liners, pieced from large balloons
    and two man rubber boats
He also tried a matching pair
    of bladders from two goats.

He reasoned he should also test
    a variety of gasses
For insulating qualities
    to satisfy the masses
Freon, neon, helium
    CO_2 to name a few
He mix-match gas and liners
    to see how each would do.

He then commissioned Ralph the cook
    who owned a harness shop
To sew five hundred pairs of boots
    sometimes for days nonstop
He had them done by deadline time
    before they headed forth
Where they sold the inventory
    in deer camps throughout the North.

But Barney'd gotten greedy and
    had sold out every pair
He never even held some back
    so he'd have boots to wear
On opener, he wore the boots
    that he'd worn many times
But with them drenched in mink oil
    they seemed to work just fine.

A little chilled so Barney wandered
    back to camp at nine
Where angry crowds had gathered
    and stood waiting there in line
Clenching boots they'd bought from him
    irate and looking mean
Shouting ugly comments
    making gestures quite obscene.

They screamed their tales of woe demanding
    justice <u>must</u> be done
Barney had to face them
    for he had nowhere to run
"You're a menace to society,
    you and your deranged shoe
There's laws made to protect us
    from the awful likes of you."

"You've ruined our season opener
    with your boots pumped full of air"
The general mood among the group
    was one of deep despair.

Big Ed from down the road a ways
    could not have been much madder
He'd bought the pair of Barney's boots
    that were lined with old goat bladders
They'd done their job, held water back
    Then weakened till they broke
They suddenly, just let her go
    and both his feet were soaked

Now Stubby bought a mismatch pair
    the left foot filled with freon
The right although it felt the same
    was pumped plum full of neon
His 'lectric socks, they shorted out
    which caused the sparks to fly
His left foot froze, his right foot flashed
    he never did know why.

Even Weak-Eyes, from his camp
    had bought a mismatched pair
Filled with Nitrous-helium
    instead of real air
He'd warmed himself beside a fire
    the nitrous gas did leak
He giggled as he floated by
    suspended by his feet.

And one poor guy, whose boot was filled
    with chlorine gas quite green
Was raving like a lunatic
    and causing quite a scene
"That gas escaped and killed my buck
    it could be me instead,
One sniff, he did four cartwheels
    and then fell over dead."

The saddest case that Barney saw
    was one poor guy he knew
The crowd was pointing fingers
    and in unison said, "Pew"
His sulfur and dioxide gas
    it's smell of rotten eggs
Had ruptured out the liner
    and was leaking from his leg.

Barney wasn't stupid
     and he knew he'd seen enough
He'd have to pacify the crowd
     before things got too rough
Barney turned and raced to town
     to float a short term loan
And mortgaged almost everything
     he even <u>thought</u> he owned.

He bought back every pair of boots
     The price paid back in full
And Weak-Eyes asked for interest
     cause he thought he had some pull
The crowd dispersed, and there was Barney
     almost like before
Standing in his tattered boots,
     happy, but still poor.

HUNTER HINT

{ **Avoid noise while walking by selecting trails, easing off brush with your hands, going around it, crawling through it, etc.** }

The Snake©

1993   Mert Cowley

For years the guys in camp had heard
Old Wilbur's tales, quite absurd
He told of bucks he claimed to see
From off his stand high up a tree.

At first they listened quite intent
To how Old Wilbur's day had went
They envied all the bucks he'd see
While hunting from his deer stand tree.

But then one day the truth came out
While in his woods they walked about
They came upon Will up his tree
Sleeping soundly as could be.

That night as they all sat around
And told of what they'd seen or found
Old Wilbur gave himself away
Telling what he'd seen that day.

The gang they asked him, "At what time?"
The bucks had passed that tree he'd climbed
He paused a moment, then said "Ten"
That's when quite sound asleep he'd been.

Next fall the gang said, "We will try,
To fix Old Wilbur for his lie
"We'll get him good, let's plan to make
A shovel-tailed white snow snake."

Weak-Eyes said, "I have at home
Some surplus hunks of styrofoam
If carved with care and glued to shape
Would make one <u>super</u> white snow snake
Fred spoke up, "I have a drawer
With several dozen teeth or more
And beady eyes of proper shape
That just belong on such a snake."
The gang right then and there appoints
Big Ralph to find some old U-joints
The snake quite lifelike, then could crawl
and wiggle through the brush and all.

They gathered up the things with speed
Including one snow scoop they'd need
And took it all to Barney's shed
To build a snake Old Wilbur'd dread.

The snake they built was long and lean
Construction done to make it mean
Its flattened head and narrow snout
Its tongue that flickered in and out
Its beady eye's that seemed to stare
Its mouth two nasty fangs did wear
Built to move at any rate
Its back could then articulate
Its tail came not to a point
It wore a shovel at this joint
And painted white, enough off so
The snake stood out against the snow.

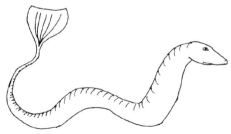

They knew that Wilbur it would fool
When Barney's wife, against his rule
Did peek inside the shed one day
And promptly fainted dead away.

The day before old Will would sit
They took their snake, positioned it
Some distance out from Wilbur's stand
Right where an old deer trail ran
And tied it to Ralph's muskie rod
The signal was, when Norm would nod
Big Ralph would reave, and set the hook
The shaking brush would make Will look.

Next morning it was not quite ten
When Wilbur checked his watch again
He placed his rifle 'crossed his lap
And closed his eyes, to take a nap.

Norm in hiding, gave his nod
So Ralph leaned back on his casting rod
And to the snake vibrations went
Through the monofilament.

His ears were trained to pick up sound
Alert of anything around
The brush was cracking! He's AWAKE!
To see the outline, of a snake.

He sat at first in silent awe
And stared intent at what he saw
He didn't dare to scream or shake
He might be spotted by the snake.

Then he thought, "I'll shoot that snake.
Oh what a trophy it will make
The way it's shaped, and easy drag
Back at the shack, then I can brag."

But then he thought, "what if I miss?
That snake will have me in one hiss
Oh what a tasty snack I'd make
My end would come, with a white snow snake."

The snake began to slither by
And Wilbur thought, "Why didn't I,
Bring my camera, I could take
Some proof there is a white snow snake.

The snake was gone but left its mark
For Will stayed put till after dark
"It's safe," he thought and did indeed
Race to his truck at breakneck speed.

Back at camp the gang did sit
When Will walked in "Well, what'd ya get?"
Will said, "It's hard for me to say,
I didn't see a thing today."

Each season now, the gang believes
Old Wilbur when he starts to leave
"Today I'll watch from off my stand"
As he goes with his camera, in his hand.

{ **Be absolutely certain of your target before shooting, and know what lies between you and the target and beyond.** }

Strange
But
True

Strange But True

Names have been omitted. They might still be around.

It was back in the 50's when one member of a gang from Ridgeland was so hungover in the morning, that his nephew handed him a Daisy Red Ryder as he headed out the door to his stand.
It was noon before the guy even noticed.

*   *   *   *   *

Back in the days of metal leg tags, a Ridgeland hunter reportedly shot a buck already tagged, healed over from the previous year.

*   *   *   *   *

From the Glenwood, WI. area:
Back in the early 1930's, Marvin had just purchased a new car before season. Those were the days when they used alcohol in the radiators for antifreeze. Marv and his hunting buddy parked the car and took off for their stands. Marv had only gone a short distance and started worrying about the radiator freezing on his new car. He walked back to the car, took a horsehide blanket out of the backseat, then draped it over the radiator.
A couple of hours later when his buddy came out of the woods, he mistook the blanket for a deer and promptly shot two bullet holes through the radiator.

*   *   *   *   *

The old trick of putting a microphone behind the seat in the ladies room and then saying "look out for the fresh paint. I'm working in here" at just the right moment isn't a new trick. The same thing worked well in a deer camp up north.

Beneath the seat of a two-holer they placed a walkie-talkie. Early next morning while it was still pitch black outside, this campmate took off on a 50 yard dash to the outhouse. He made it, and rushed in. At precisely the right moment a voice said, "Get out and wait your turn, we were here first."

Needless to say some time was spent putting the door to the outhouse on.

Note: One thing about pulling off a prank in deer camp. With the passage of time, even the victim begins to laugh about it.

*   *   *   *   *

It was back in 1930 that Walt Kittleson got the horns from a buck before he shot it.

Walt and his cousin were making firewood one morning when they happened across a nice shed laying in the snow. The shed was so freshly dropped that a visible trail of blood led away from the shed. Being young and inquisitive, Walt and his cousin took up the trail. They followed it for a short distance and came upon the other shed, and the tracks of a now bald buck.

The boys took the sheds back to the house to show Walt's uncle. His uncle's words were, "that buck will grow a good many sets of horns before you boys catch up to him." That of course was all it took. The boys each grabbed a rifle and took off on the buck's trail.

The buck soon knew he was being followed and proceeded to lead the boys through every swamp and tangle it could find, but the boys were not about to give up. It was getting late in the afternoon and still no buck when Walt decided rather than chase the buck, they would work the buck with the wind. It worked. The buck broke out of the swamp and was dropped.

The boys proved a point.

You can have your bucks horns, and eat it too.

* * * * *

A hunter from the Hayward area once shot a buck underwater.

He was on a drive in the Mondovi area. A buck was seen running into the woods they were driving, but it wouldn't come out. Several attempts from different directions proved futile and they were about to give up.

This hunter, hot and wet anyway, decided to walk right down the middle of a small stream to get back out to the road. He was walking in the shallows and as he worked around the edge of a deep hole on the bend, he spotted the tip of an antler sticking out of the water. He stared and made out the end of a deer's nose just above the surface of the water. He aimed and fired where he figured the head was and that little trout stream literally erupted with buck, water, and foam. Drenched from head to toe, it took the hunter one more shot before he could claim his prize.

* * * * *

Several years ago, two hunters from the central part of the state were doing a little hunting somewhat after hours. Spotting a doe not far from the road, a well placed shot dropped it where it stood. After a quick dash through the ditch and under the fence, each grabbed a leg and headed back to the car, entrails and all. They quickly tossed it in the trunk, slammed the trunk lid, jumped in, and down the road they went.

Proud of themselves, they headed for home to complete the job. All was going well until it became increasingly difficult to keep the car on the road. It began to sway and lean as the driver fought to keep it between the ditches. Suddenly the backseat was kicked into the passenger department and they realized the problem. They now had one fully alive, very irritated deer in the trunk. Slamming on the brakes they skidded to the side of the road. By then, the surface of the trunk lid was showing dents from being kicked from the inside. There was only one thing to do, open the trunk.

The key was turned, the lid flew open and suddenly these hunters of the night had a face full of escaping deer to contend with. Both were knocked to the ground suffering minor cuts and scrapes in the melee. The deer escaped none the worse for wear.

Revenge is mine, sayeth the doe.

* * * * *

The Hooded Man

This story of the hooded man has circulated for many years now, up here in the Northwoods. It was an especially cold winter day that this fellow, dressed in a hooded snowmobile suit made his way to a local tavern at days end.

He had been there about an hour and both he and his hooded suit, began to thaw out. It was then, that many of the patrons began to detect a rather foul odor throughout the tavern.

Time passed and the smell continued to get worse, and seemed to be concentrated in one area of the tavern, near where the man in the hooded suit stood.

Working their way through the crowd, two men finally discovered the source of the problem as they peered into the hood hanging on the back of "The Hooded Man."

It was obvious that some time during the course of the day, he had made an emergency stop, and it wasn't at the bank. He had however left his deposit in the hood of his suit. He, his hood, and his deposit quite soon departed.

We thank you for the memories pal. "Hats off to you."

HUNTER HINT

{ Learn how to use compass and never go hunting without it, no matter how well you think you know the area. }

Jim Forster of Menomonie, Wisconsin contributed the following stories. These stories of Jim and his father Harry are prime examples which illustrate the bond that develops between family members who spend a great deal of time together in the outdoors.

Jim, Nathan, Harry Forster.

Too Close for Comfort

When Chuck and I were young before we were in school (probably 4 & 5 years old), Dad dropped us off about a mile from the farm. He went back to his deer stand to wait for us to make a drive. We started following a fox track, thinking we were on a deer track. We followed it all the way to Dad's stand. The funny part was a deer was following us. It was so close to us Dad couldn't shoot. Neither Chuck nor I knew the deer was behind us.

* * * * *

What's Up Doc?

Dad took us out to look for our stands, the Sunday before deer season. Mom was supposed to go to Sacred Heart Hospital at 4:00 p.m. that day (she was having surgery). Dad was driving through the Chippewa bottoms and got the car stuck. (He was mowing down willows that looked big as trees and taller than the car.) It was starting to get late so he decided he'd hike home and we could get a tractor from the farmer to get us out. When he finally got home he was pooped, late, and Mom was furious. When they got to the hospital he looked so bad the nurse made a mistake and got a wheelchair for him instead of Mom. Then she really was mad. She never let him forget it.

* * * * *

Nothin' could be finer than to stand there in a liner.

This story is about my father-in-law Brownie Lahm. I fell in love with him almost as much as I did my wife. He was a deer hunting and fishing companion for 10 years. We lost him in 1988 or 89 to cancer.

One of his last seasons was bitterly cold. That opening Sunday was well below zero. We went on stand about 6:30 a.m. By 9:00 a.m. I was froze to the bone. I walked out to our arranged meeting place. There stood Brownie looking colder than I felt. He said, "You know, when I put my boots on this morning I told my son Buzz they felt awful loose but I said "Well, better too loose than too tight." You know, I forgot to put the felt liners in.' Now that's tough, on stand for 3 hours at probably 15 below with no liners in your snowmobile boots.

*   *   *   *   *

The Last Buck

This was Dad's last deer season (1991). He was 80 years old. Because of all the snow I couldn't get him back to his stand so I put him in the pine trees behind the old log house. I went over the hill to sit. It was really cold. After about one hour I heard 3 shots. I waited awhile and then walked over the hill to see what he got. When I got there he had a puzzled look on his face. I said "Well, did you get one?" He said he wasn't sure. So then he told me his story. It seems a doe came through that he missed broadside at about 10 yards. He was feeling bad about it and when he looked up he saw an 8 pt. buck with his nose to the ground. He was so taken up with the scent of the doe he never saw Dad. Dad aimed at him right between the eyes but when he shot, the buck turned and bolted. Then Dad aimed for his "ass." I asked Dad where he thought he hit him. He said in the head and the "ass." I never heard of such a thing. I found the blood trail and 60 yards later a nice 8 point buck. He was right. He'd hit him just below the eyes (it came out the jaw so it didn't do any real damage). When he hit it in the rear end it severed a main artery. That's why the deer didn't go very far. I have the horns and best memory you could ever have of your best friend.

Harry Forster, Tom Thornton, Amanda Forster, Jim Forster, and John Koll.

Quoting from Jim Forsters letter

Thanks for considering these stories for your book. These two men were dearly loved and are greatly missed. I'm blessed however to have a lifetime of wonderful memories.

In closing, Mert—I wish you could have known what a great story teller Dad was. People would sit for hours listening to his stories.

In fact, he was telling the nurse about his deer hunting stand when he died.

Thanks,
Jim Forster

Of all the guys that are in camp

Only one will be your Dad

This is the contents of a personal letter written by Bob Traun to a friend who had recently lost his father. It has a message for all of us who some-day may have to face the same situation.

Courtesy - Bob Traun
Deer and Deer Hunting

The Hunt Continues

Dear Doug, old friend,

I think I know how you feel to-day, on the eve of your first deer season without your father, your son Brian's grandfather. I lost my father 11 years ago and, although it hasn't been the same, I am struck now with mixed feelings and perhaps a different perspective than I had in November 1980.

I knew it would be tough that first year, but the older generation of hunters in camp, my dad's friends, really helped me remember him in a way that brought some good memories. And on that opening day, my younger brother, Jim, shot his first deer and suddenly I be-came the father. I was so proud for him! For the first time in my life I understood how Dad must have felt when I shot my first deer in 1968.

Some year, maybe this one, you will have that same opportunity with Brian.

I will always remember the first time my dad called me a man, and treated me as one. It was my 16th year, my first time in the deer camp. I realized that I was being invited into this close fraternity of Dad's friends, and their sons, and it was something special. I began then to understand the unique bond that deer hunting partners feel for each other.

Today I can acknowledge that the loss of a parent is a natural thing, perhaps as difficult to accept as it is inevitable. You were the child, and now the parent. You hunted with your grandfather, and he passed on. Now Brian's grandfather has passed on. This is the first year Brian will hunt alone in a stand. You see, he's growing to be a man, too.

As you feel the loss, think of how your dad would have wanted you to react. Probably not with much sadness, but rather a celebration of his life, the traditions of deer camp, and hunts long past. Would he expect you to carry on in these same traditions? Absolutely. So have fun, tell a few deer stories, and remember days forever gone.

You may also find comfort in thinking about it this way: The way I figure, our dads met last spring up there in the Great Deer Shack, and have been swapping lies and making plans for the fall hunt ever since. So while you and I are freezing in the cold November woods, our fathers will be sitting in their deer stands, where the winds blow gently, the snowflakes fall softly, and where some day, we can all hunt together again.

Your friend,
Bob

A Deerhunter's Prayer

Lord, when each season's over
   how I hate to see it pass
For every year, I always fear
   that it could be my last

Lord, I know it may sound selfish
   And to some it may seem wrong
But let Heaven's woods be full of bucks
With a season all year long.

—Cowley '92

The Future of Deer Hunting

To ensure that the sport of deer hunting will always have a future, we, the hunters of the present must assume a responsibility. It is our duty to see that hunters of the future are initiated into the sport of deer hunting in the same manner accorded us by those who were before us.

It is our duty to present hunting as a privilege that must be respected.

It is our duty to teach new hunters many things, for they have much to learn.

They must be willing to start very young whenever possible so they become confident of themselves.

Dan Lee   1961

Joey Cowley - 1989
Age 3 years

Mike Kramshuster   1989

Joey and "Grampy" Mert
1993

They must learn how to blend ways of the past with the ways of their own times.

They must learn how to hunt both independently, and as a member of a group.

Joey Cowley and his new 243 Remington
Slide action. Presented to him June, 1993.

They must learn the proper handling of their rifle, and the limits of its use.

They must learn to be certain of their target and to look at what is beyond.

They must learn to respect their fellow hunters in many ways: their feelings, their rights, their hunts, and their land.

1974 David & Dan Cowley, and
Honee with Dan's first pheasant.

Joey Cowley with Grampy's
partridge   1989
Age 3½ years

They must learn to respect their quarry both dead <u>and</u> alive.
They must be taught to respect themselves as hunters so at the end of a hunt they feel good about what they've done. If they have done their best, if they have used every skill they have learned and have tried their hardest, they are successful, whether they filled their tag or not.

Joey and his Dad Dan - 1989
Beatin' the brush for a bird

Joey and "Grampy Mert" - 1989
Checking out the deer stands.

<u>We</u> as the teachers, must be an example for those who are watching and learning, for they will model themselves after us.

Dan and Dave at a Buck Rub   1980

<u>We</u> must learn to take time to show these future hunters the little things of life, that often we have nearly forgotten, or now take for granted. They are things they will learn to appreciate.

Dave and Dan near the Pearly Swamp Camp - Burnett Co., WI   1980

If <u>we</u> the hunters they depend on will do this, we may leave quite confident that the tradition of deer hunting will continue.

Which of the two is Greater?

Is it:

The Anticipation of young who will go on their first hunt in the morning,

-or-

The Deliberation of the old who must decide if this morning's hunt is his last?

{ Never use your riflescope to identify movements in the woods. Use binoculars first, and don't replace them with the scope unless you intend to shoot. }

Deer Hunting Language
A Glossary of Common terms

Deer hunters have a language all their own. Deer language is basic English combined with a myriad of terms which tend to have multiple meanings and connotations that only deer hunters can understand and relate to. In order to become a true deer hunter, one must not only be able to understand deer hunting terminology but must be able to use it fluently in order to communicate with others.

A glossary of terms used in deer language has been included in this text. Deer words are not only defined here, but a concise example of their proper use has been included. By using this glossary, a hunter should be able to walk into any deer hunting camp and speak deer language.

Words have been listed in alphabetical order for the convenience of the hunter. There is no doubt several terms have been errantly missed or purposely omitted. Feel free to add your own.

ace -

   a) One who is an expert.
Weak-Eyes is no ace. He just missed another buck.

   b) Playing cards having but one dot.
Ralph took the pot with a full house, aces high.

acorn -

   a) Fruit or nut of the oak tree.
After seeing nothing all day, Bear Breath figured they must be eating acorns.

   b) A growth on a hunter's toe.
Acorn which developed on Willie's toe had him limping all season.

alcohol -

   a) A highly inflammable liquid necessary to preheat the generator for many fuel oil heaters.
Barney spilled alcohol on the floor and had to stamp the fire out.

   b) A set of instructions given to a campmate named Al after he just dropped his fifth buck.
Alcohol your own buck out of the swamp.

back -

   a) A region of the body surrounding the spine.
Dan and Dave always get backaches when a buck must be tied to the pole.

   b) To return.
Don't look now, the Warden's coming back.

back up -

   a) To go in reverse.
Willie backed up and drove over his rifle.

   b) To force smoke into a room.
Norm closed the damper too much and the stove backed up.

   c) To return to position.
Your cheap rope broke. We've got to hang my buck back up.

back track -

a) To try and follow one's own footsteps.
Willie back tracked trying to find where he'd left his credit card.

b) To try and follow someone else's tracks.
Duff knew he had hit the buck, so he back tracked to where it had stood.

c) An imprint in the snow.
When Barney fell off the edge of the porch into the snow he left a back track.

Bambi -

a) The infant stage of a deer.
I told you not to use a 24 power scope. You just got a Bambi.

b) Name for a go-go dancer.
Weak-Eyes was a believer when Bambi danced.

bear -

a) A large mammal covered with coarse hair.
Ralph leaned too far forward, and fell right into the bear den.

b) A gruff surly person.
Clarence is a bear when you wake him at four in the morning.

c) To put up with, to tolerate.
"That's ten times you told me how you got your buck. I can't bear to hear it again."

Bear-Breath -

a) A foul odor exhaled while breathing.
By the third day of camp, most of its members had bear-breath.

b) A nickname.
By the third day of the season, anyone in camp is Bear-Breath.

c) Normal exhaling by a bear.
Joey could feel the bear's breath on his neck as he ran for the shack.

beaver -

a) A large furred creature which inhabits areas of water.
On opening morning, Ralph found that a beaver had chewed down his popple tree stand.

b) A heavy woolen cloth (straight out of the dictionary folks).
Martha didn't speak to Weak-Eyes for several days after he told her he'd gone to town and bought some beaver.

beaver dam -

a) A construction of sticks and mud which creates an impoundment of water.
The newly constructed beaver dam had flooded Norm's favorite buck swamp.

b) A reverse curse, often spoken when chilled.
"Beavers dam" John shouted as he fell off the dam into the icy waters.

belt -

a) An area of heavy snows.
John and Terry, hunting in the snow belt, were up their waists in fluff.

b) An item of apparel placed through loops of one's pants.
Ralph's pants kept dropping to his ankles as he dragged the buck out with his belt.

c) A drink.
After missing two bucks, Bill decided to have a belt.

brown -

a) A dullish color.
Larry's wife complained about his brown colored under wear when he got home from camp.

b) Name for a deer.
"Today boys, brown is down."

brush -

a) A growth of small shrubs, usually quite dense.
Dan put his head down and stumbled through the brush.

b) To rub against.
Frank positioned himself in a doorway so the "exotic dancers" had to brush past him on their way to the dance floor.

brush buck -

a) Male of the deer family which inhabits dense growths of shrubs.
Larry brought in a swamp buck, Pete got himself an old brush buck.

b) A member of the deer family dishonestly acquired for camp meat.
Many years ago it was a common practice for each camp to have a brush buck. (This is no longer a suggested practice for both financial and ethical reasons.)

Buck -

a) Male of the deer family.
That twelve year old kid got a bigger buck than you did.

b) Paper of monetary value.
"If you're still in, you'll have to sweeten the pot a buck."

buck fever -

a) A temporary ailment often brought on by the very sight of an antlered buck.
He had such a case of buck fever that he couldn't even shoot.

b) An ailment brought on by severe changes in temperature or resulting from heavy participation in a rut.
"I just want to stay here in my bed today Rudolph. I was out all night and have come down with a case of buck fever."

bung hole -

a) Hole in the side of a barrel.
When the cork blew, Frank, who was facing the bung hole, was nearly drowned in a deluge of beer.

b) An anatomical term describing the vent found at the rear portion of a deer.
"Look at the meat you ruined. You shot it right in the bung hole."

bunk -

a) A bed set against the wall like a shelf.
Bear Breath fell out of his bunk around midnight.

b) To sleep in rough quarters.
"You look like you've had it. Why don't you bunk here tonight."

c) Insincere talk, baloney, or malarkey.
"I think all those deer you claim to see is a lot of bunk."

burn -

a) The site of an old forest fire.
The blueberries were thick up on the burn.

b) Process of oxidation caused by severe heat.
"Oh! Oh! The oven's at 550. Boy, did that turkey ever burn. Let's head to the Log Cabin Store for pizza."

c) To become irritated.
If you really want to burn a campmate, make them late to their stand opening morning.

camp -

a) To temporarily take up residence.
Many of the old hunters used to pitch a tent and camp in the woods.

b) A permanent structure.
Whenever Weak-Eyes and Martha argue, he jumps into the car and heads for camp.

clip -

a) A metallic device whose primary purpose is to hold a reserve supply of shells.
"Come on you guys, help me look for my clip."

b) A rate of travel.
When Willie missed the first shot, the buck took off at a rapid clip.

cookie -

a) A food material baked of flour dough often with nuts or fruits contained within.
Joey's lunch was nothing but crumbs when he forgot and sat on his cookies.

b) Nickname for the head chef of the camp.
The new guy made a smart remark about the gravy and we all had to sit on the cookie till we got him calmed down.

c) To throw, to toss, to upchuck, to hurl.
At the taste of Ralph's gravy, Barney ran for the door and tossed his cookies.

death trap -

a) A confined area of a woods. A deer funnel.
They took two bucks and a doe at the death trap.

b) A confined area of wooden construction.
Everyone in camp calls the outhouse "The Death Trap" after Ralph's been in there.

dingle -

a) The tone from a brass bell.
The dingle stopped when Norm fired. He was now the proud owner of a goat.

b) A small, fur-covered berry which appears in quantity in late November.
Lawrence said, "the time had come to head home and pick some dingle berries."

dish/dishes -   a)   A flat, usually round utensil of glass or paper whose purpose is to hold food.
Dave said he didn't mean to drop the dish, but it was hot and slippery.

    b)   A slang term used to describe a lady.
Weak-Eyes gets kinda hot and a little slippery himself when he spots a good looking dish.

dish cloth/dish rag

    a)   A cloth like material purchased for the sole purpose of washing and or drying dishes.

-or-

    b)   Any old cloth like material used to wash or dry dishes.
The boys were using a T-shirt for a dish cloth, and an old pair of shorts for a dish rag.

does -   a)   The female of the deer family, often referred to as baldies.
"Saw a lot of does this morning but no bucks."

    b)   A way of speaking.
Ralph said, "get does things off my counter, I'm trying to fix supper."

drive -   a)   A group effort used to move deer.
Bill got lost again and messed up another drive.

    b)   To travel, to transport.
Here, I think you'd better drive.

drop/dropped - a)   To lose hold of.
It was a good thing Pete's rifle wasn't loaded when he dropped it from his tree stand.

    b)   To release purposely.
Ted raced to the nearest jack pine, hung his jacket on it, and then dropped his Malones.

drippings/droppings -

    a) Fats and juices produced by the cooking of meats and fowl.
Willie added raisins to the drippings and made a delicious stuffing for the turkey.

    b) Fecal materials vented by a deer.
Little Ernie saw a prank in the making as he compared raisins and droppings.

drop tines -

    a) Strange growths and configurations found on many non-typical racks.
Kirk's 17 pointer had two beautiful drop tines off each beam.

    b) The result of a mishandled fork.
When the fork slipped out of Rick's hand the dropped tines stuck right in his little toe.

fender -

    a) The metal covering over the wheel of many older vehicles.
Dan and his dad drove down the road with a buck tied to each of the front fenders.

    b) An instrument.
The lead guitar in the Country band was a Fender from the 50's.

flag -

    a) A cloth with color or pattern standing for a country.
As part of the morning ritual, most camps have its members face the flag and repeat an oath.

    b) What you usually see on a deer.
The only thing I saw today was three flags.

gut -

    a) The abdominal region.
No more liver, beans, or onions. I have a real gut ache.

    b) Slang term used by Ralph.
I gut me a buck this morning.

gut pile -   a) The abdominal contents from a deceased deer.
"Keep your eyes open for a warm gut pile and grab the heart and liver."

b) The assemblage of guts.
When four members of the camp fell off the edge of the porch, it made for a real gut pile.

horns/horn -   a) The calcium growth protruding from the base of a buck's skull.
With both horns shot off, you'll have to use your quota tag.

b) An instrument of sound.
"Lay on the horn again, he can't be that deaf."

horny -   a) A multitude of horn-like projections near the base of a buck's horns.
"Now there's a horny buck."

Hunter's ball -   a) A festive occasion usually held on the second Saturday night of season.
Weak-Eyes, you made a fool of yourself at the Hunter's ball again this year.

b) A type of football played on Thanksgiving Day.
When we're done eating, let's run over to the Fishbowl and watch the game on wide screen T.V.

jerky -   a) A dried meaty material that all deer hunters think they should have.
"I've eaten so much jerky, my jaws ache and my tongue's all dried out.

b) A manner of driving.
Slow down on these logging roads, it's gettin' way too jerky.

kitty -

a) A pot or a pool.
   Ante up, the kitty's light.

b) A small member of the cat family.
   "I don't care if that is your kid's kitty, keep it away from the buck pole."

c) Weak-Eye's favorite Go-Go Dancer.
   "I could sit here and watch Kitty all night.

Log -

a) Something to make a fire out of.
   "It's your turn to get up and put a log on the fire."

b) A large portion of a tree.
   "I wonder who put this log across the trail? Now I can't drive back to my stand."

c) To make record of, a journal.
   "I mean it. If you write that about me in the Log, I'll rip the page out when you're not looking."

long john(s) -

a) A tall member of the camp.
   "I wouldn't sleep there. The bunk's not that long John."

b) A type of pastry.
   "Look, I found a sack of long johns. Are they from this year, or last year?"

c) A type of clothing.
   Ralph didn't think it was funny. Somebody had sewed the back of his long johns shut.

lost -

a) Something misplaced.
   "Help, I've lost my back tag.

b) Someone misplaced.
   Willy seems to get lost every year.

moss -

a) A type of green vegetation found on a tree.
My grandpa always told me, "You're never lost. Moss always grows on the north side of a tree

b) A type of green vegetation found on all sides of a tree.
"We're lost. Look here, moss, moss, moss, and moss."

mount -

a) A way of preserving one's trophy.
"You're not serious are you? You're going to mount that spike?"

b) A metal object which attaches the scope of a rifle.
"No wonder I missed. My mount's loose."

old timer -

a) An aged buck.
"Look at the size of this track. That has to be an Old Timer."

b) Senior member of the camp.
"Don't ask me what to do about hemorrhoids. Ask one of the old timers."

c) A counting device.
"Well it happened again. The turkey is burned to a crisp. That old timer on the stove must be shot."

opener -

a) The first day of deer season.
"Quick! Everybody up! The alarm clock quit. We'll miss the opener."

b) A metal device used to remove caps from bottles.
"Look, openers don't just disappear. Where'd you set it?"

poach -
    a) A means of cooking eggs.
'Ralph, I said I wanted my eggs poached, not boiled to death."

    b) Words spoken by an inebriated campmate.
"Wow it's slippery out there. I almost went off the poach."

pot -
    a) A cooking device.
"Here, scrub it again. The beans burned to the bottom of the pot."

    b) A collection of money.
"What do you mean, you won the pot? I've got aces over eights."

pool -
    a) Body of water, often collecting behind a dam.
"You're the third guy that fell off the beaver dam today. We should call this the fool pool."

    b) A stake played for in some games.
"What do you mean you're not going in the buck pool this year. You won it last year."

    c) A game played with balls and cue stick.
"It's raining too hard to hunt today. Let's go play some pool."

    d) To put money together for common advantage.
"If we pool our money together, we can buy enough gas to make it home."

rattle -
    a) To clatter together.
T-Bone required a bandaid after smashing his thumb trying to rattle a buck.

    b) To become shaken.
"How can you let a little spike like that completely rattle you?"

rifle -

    a) A gun with spiral grooves shot from the shoulder.
"Who in the 'H' do you think you are, Rifleman? Aim your rifle next time."

    b) To search.
Shorty rifled through his suitcase looking for his license.

rut -

    a) A time of great sexual frenzy.
"You're sick. You'd rather be up north for the rut, than home here with me and the kids. Am I right?"

    b) A groove created in a road or trail.
"Watch out. If it drops in that rut we'll be here for awhile. Watch Out!"

running board -

    a) A rubber covered metal platform connected to the fenders of an older car.
"Ralph, it has to be those onions. You smell so bad, I'm riding home on the running board.

    b) A strenuous type of exercise.
Running board is what your not doing with a bear three feet behind you.

running full bore -

    a) This is what you're doing with a bear behind you.

runs -

    a) Narrow grassy pathways made by denizens of a swamp.
Norm sat all day watching several runs before he realized it was a snowshoe rabbit's.

    b) With great speed and agility.
Seth figured he had the runs from too much fresh venison.

season -

a) Time of pursuit.
Well, another season over and no bucks.

b) To flavor.
"Ralph, is there a reason, you don't season?"

shack -

a) Common name for a dwelling whose primary purpose is for hunting.
"But Honey, I have to go up to the shack. This is our yearly work weekend."

shack up -

a) To construct a dwelling for the purpose of hunting.
"Well boys, we finally got the shack up."

shot -

a) To bring down.
"Mike shot the smallest deer I've ever seen."

b) Tired, pooped, worn out.
"I'm not going anywhere tonight, I'm shot."

c) A small glass container.
Norval chipped his tooth with a shot glass.

sight -

a) To view or to see.
"I set here all day with not a deer in sight."

b) Metal device used in aiming.
"Take me to town. I just broke my front sight."

smoke -

a) To burn tobacco.
He wonders why he sees no deer. All he does all day is sit and smoke.

b) To beat in cards.
"How do you like this hand? Boy did I smoke your butt."

c) To leave in great haste.
The old buck dug in and started to smoke.

d) A by-product of burning wood.
"Open the damper, or you'll smoke us out."

snow -

a) A white fluffy material one prays for.
"Boys, all I want is three inches of fresh snow on opening morning."

b) A white fluffy material one prays not to get.
"Boys, I don't want it to snow now. I have 300 miles to drive tonight."

snowshoes -

a) Name for the varying hare, denizen of the coniferous swamp.
Doesn't look like we'll get any deer. We may as well bump off a few snowshoes.

b) A wooden framed, leather laced device used by man to walk on snow.
"Help me stand up and get these damn snowshoes off my feet. I almost broke my ankle."

snort -

a) The rapid exhaling of air through the nostril of a deer.
"Listen, I think I hear a buck snort."

b) A sound somewhat resembling that made by a buck.
"Del, was that you that just snorted?"

c) A form of liquid refreshment.
"Boy, Bill's sure got a snort full tonight."

stand -

a) To remain motionless in an upright position.
"Hurry up and get moving. I can't stand here all day."

b) To remain motionless while in a sitting position.
"I'm going to sit on my stand this morning."

c) A location or position.
"I'm going out and check over my stand."

b) To tolerate.
"How can you stand to stand on your stand all day?"

stew -

    a) A name.
        "Well Stew, did you see anything?"

    b) A spot or condition, a mess.
        "If that isn't your tag you're carrying boy,
        you're in a real stew."

    c) A type of food served in camp.
        "Anybody else think this stew tastes a little
        funny."

swamp -

    a) To scrub or wash.
        "I'll do the dishes and clean off the counter,
        you swamp the floor."

    b) To become buried in.
        "Boy am I glad to be in camp. We were just
        swamped at work."

    c) A damp, low lying region.
        "<u>You</u> drive the swamp this time. It was up to
        my rear in water last time."

tangle -

    a) To hang up or obstruct.
        Willie ripped his brand new wool pants in the
        blackberry tangle.

    b) To twist or twine together.
        Fred's armpit was a virtual tangle by the end
        of the fourth day of hunting.

tote -

    a) To carry.
        "Here, you take the drag rope, I'll tote the
        guns."

    b) A narrow woodland roadway.
        "It looks like this tote road ends right up there.
        Where do we turn around?"

track -
   a) An imprint of an animal's foot.
"Hey, that looks like a bear track right on top of your track. Listen! Did you hear that?"

   b) To follow with reason.
"Looks like a buck, I'm going to track it all day."

   c) To follow for no good reason.
"That's our track. We've walked in a circle. We're lost."

tracking snow -
   a) A thin layer of fresh snow.
"Gee, I wish we'd get a tracking snow tonight."

   b) A thick layer of fresh snow.
"I don't care if we did get 18 inches last night. I'm still going hunting."

trail -
   a) A path through the woods.
"That's no deer trail you're on, that a rabbit's boy."

   b) To follow.
"I had to give up. I couldn't trail it anymore."

trapdoor
   a) The door which covers a secured area beneath the floor.
"Next time, if you're going to monkey around, close the trapdoor before somebody else falls in.

   b) Flap on the back of long johns.
"How come you're back in camp so early? No, I didn't sew it shut."

weasel -
   a) A small, quick, sly, 4-legged mammal.
I saw a weasel run into the woodpile today.

   b) A sly quick two-legged animal.
"Get away from our woodpile you dirty weasel. Go cut your own firewood."

233

weasel-eyed -   a)   The look of a small, quick, sly mammal.
Norton always got a little weasel-eyed the night before the opener.

whack/whacked -

    a)   To bring about the demise of. (See greased.)
Weak-Eyes whacked a doe.

    b)   To strike.
Kitty, Bambi and Bonnie all whacked Weak-Eyes when he mentioned the <u>word</u> dough.

wheel -   a)   To turn, to spin.
When the buck saw me, it wheeled and ran up the hill.

    b)   A means of control.
"Look out, we're going into a spin! You better let me take the wheel."

work -   a)   Hard labor or chore.
"Boy, dragging a buck over dry ground is a lot of work."

    b)   Occupation, business.
"Call my boss and tell him I'm too sick to come to work. No, tell him I'm lost in the woods and presumed dead. Tell him anything. Tell him I'm having a great time deer hunting and wish he was here. Tell him . . . . "

Words you might wish to add for your own camp

_____

_____

_____

_____

_____

_____

_____

_____

_____

_____

_____

_____

_____

_____

_____

Tuesday evening after season -

Dear Log,

Members present and accounted for:
Barlow "Buck" Malone
Gomer "Gut Shot" Johnson
Calvin "Bear Breath" Calhoun
Wilbur "Weak Eyes" Sweeny
Bernard "Barney" Oleson
Ralph "The Cookie" Carlson

It has been a tradition for many years now, that the members of The Pearly Swamp Gang assemble over at Weak-Eyes' house for one last meeting of the year. The evenings activities usually include cutting up the deer we have, then planning our annual member/wives Christmas party, discussing any major topics which have come up since our last meeting, and then finishing the evenin off with several frying pans full of fried backstrap and tenderloin, onions, and mushrooms. This meeting was no exception, save a few minor differences.

It has always been Weak-Eyes' job to see that the deer are brought in the previous evening and hung in the basement to thaw, enabling us to proceed with our chores as soon as possible. This season however, turned out to be a fluke.

We, the members of The Pearly Swamp Camp had questioned the large number of quota permits and bonus tags which the DNR had issued for our hunting area. It had been our observations since last season, that the deer numbers were way down, due to a severe winter and an overkill in the area the previous season. But who were we to question the experts? However, by the end of the season, the group had managed but one deer. We still had a great season, but I guess it turned out that _we_ were right.

At any rate, Weak-Eyes had somehow missed seeing the one deer and had forgotten to put it into the basement until an hour before the group assembled, fully prepared to get the butchering done and to close the season for another year. Ralph, of course, stood in disbelief as the frost hadn't even melted off the buck's nasal hairs yet. "Weak-Eyes" he said, "we give you one little job to do and you muffed it." Weak-Eyes just stood there, slump-shouldered and shaking his head.

It was I, Barney, who came to Weak-Eyes' defense. "Leave him alone, at least he's given us a good reason to get out of the house again this week. Let's just make the best of it and hold a formal meeting and get a few things out of the way." The group agreed and the meeting was called to order by President Barlow "the Buck" Malone.

The first order of business was the topic of Bear-Breath Calhouns brother-in-law whom he had dragged into camp as a possible new member of the Pearly Swamp Gang. It was Weak-Eyes who opened up the discussion first, his voice trembling as he described his experiences. "If that guy walks into camp next year, I'm going to have to walk out. He almost drove me nuts this year. As a hunter, he was certainly good enough and safe enough around camp, but it was his constant desire to bet that got to me. You guys have no idea what I went through. You weren't in camp with him for hours like I was. Here's a list of some of his bets I jotted down.

1) I'll bet that you have a flat tire on your truck opening morning on the way to your stand. I did.

2) I'll bet you miss the biggest buck you've ever seen, which I did.

3) I'll bet we won't see a tracking snow until seasons over, which we didn't.

4) I'll bet Ralphs gravy is bad, and Ralph I hate to tell you this, but it was.

5) I'll bet I see more deer this year than all the rest of the gang put together. He did, that's his buck we're waiting for to thaw.

6) I'll bet somebody else shoots the buck you've been trailing all day. Somebody did, you should have seen it, Old Mossy Horns himself.

7) I'll bet a red squirrel chews a hole in your brand new down sleeping bag. You fella's heard me sneezing all hours of the night. Those little feathers kept drifting up my nose.

then he started parlay betting.

8) I'll bet your scope fogs up, you have a misfire, your gun jams, and that you break through the swamp up to your neck. You guys remember what a day I had on Wednesday don't you?

9) I'll bet there's roaches under the sink, bed bugs in the mattress, and a mouse chews a hole length-ways in a loaf of bread. That's when I took some money out of the camp kitty and went to town for varmint supplies. By the way, those baby mice that mother mouse had in the loaf of bread sure were cute. I carried loaf and all out and put it under the woodpile.

239

Fellas, it was like he put a jinx on me. The worst part is, I took him up on all those bets and now I'm a little short of having enough money for Martha's Christmas present.

Following a brief discussion and no opposition, it was moved and seconded that he not be invited back next year. The gang all looked at Ralph kind of funny when he said, "Boy, I'll bet _he'll_ be surprised."

The next item on the agenda was also brought up by Weak-Eyes. It involved a complaint he had against the Post Office and some of their regulations. He felt a strong letter of disapproval should be sent to perhaps the Postmaster himself.

It seems that his mother-in-law called and said she was coming to visit and that she expected Weak-Eyes to pay her way. Weak-Eyes obliged by sending her a five dollar roll of bulk mailing stamps. The Post Office then refused to honor the stamps.

There was no further discussion other than Bear Breath's suggestion that he might try UPS. The matter was then tabled.

Weak-Eyes then requested to use the hunting shack for two weeks in July, coinciding with her visit.

The next item on the agenda centered around this past deer season itself. It was Ralph's feeling that something had to be done to let the DNR know that hunters in the North wanted something done before the entire northern deer herd had been annihilated. He started out the discussion by saying, "It looks to me like the DNR is running around in circles Lika one-armed mole." We all tended to agree with him. Gut-Shot said he figured it was time to do something when his grandson came home from school and told how he was going to pull a joke on one of his little playmates. His grandson said to the kid, "How many deer does Santa Claus have to pull his sleigh?" Everybody knows there's eight, nine if you count Rudolph. The kid says, "My Daddy told me there's a hundred twenty-one." His old man works for the DNR you know."

I quickly moved and it was seconded by Gut-Shot Johnson that Ralph be sent as our delegate to the annual spring meeting held every year at the Court-house, to discuss the rules and regulations for the upcoming year. Ralph is to suggest to the group that the DNR be immediately put in charge of mosquito control beginning this coming summer. If they control mosquitos like they control the deer herd, all the mosquitos should be eliminated within two years.

It was a unanimous vote by all members in attendance
   Weak-Eyes felt something should be done even
sooner than that. He suggested something be presented
to the DNR yet this year. It was I who remembered
that the DNR Christmas party was going to be held
at the supper club on December 19th. Maybe we
could present something to them when we had them
all in one spot.
   Weak-Eyes had been humming the tune, "My
Bonnie Lies Over the Ocean." He may have been assoc-
iating the name Bonnie with one of the girls he saw
up at the Go-Go Joint. I can't say this for certain
but at any rate it started the wheels to turn.
   "Let's write them a song! After they get done
eating, they could have a little sing-a-long with
Helga Jorgenson backing them at the piano. That put
us to thinking of some verses for our song. Weak-Eyes
ran for paper and pencils and we put together
the following song, sung to the tune of "My Bonnie
Lies Over the Ocean."

The fawn ♫ they all died in the deer yards.
The does didn't breed on the run
Tell the public the deer are still out there
We'll sell bonus tags by the ton!

Sing   Chorus:

Rolls in, Rolls in
My how the money rolls in, rolls in
Rolls in, rolls in (hold on this one)
Oh, my, how the money rolls in!

Who cares if the deer herd's depleted;
They get on the roads, anyway!
Save a tree, will the paper mills pay us?
Don't let hunters stand in our way!

Sing   Chorus.

Propose now a 16-day season
The deer lose, the DNR wins
It worked so well for us this past year
Let's do it all over again!

End by singing chorus twice.

The whole gang really got into it. Once we
had the song put together, we had to sing it several
times. The meeting had turned into a songfest.
   One of the members had the bright idea that if
we got so we sounded good enough we should cut a
record of it. We could use the profits to put a new
roof on the shack. Ralph thought it was a good idea
and said, "If the Yuppers can do it, we can too."
I suggested we use the $197.14 in the camp kitty
to promote the record.
   The meeting however, ended abruptly when Martha
stuck her head down the basement stairs and informed

243

us in no uncertain terms that she had heard enough. Our verse writing contest had gotten out of hand when some of our lyrics got a little to raunchy. We would have been all right but "Gut-Shot" always gets to loud when he tries to take over the lead. We called the contest a draw. There were no winners including the deer.

It was moved and seemded that next year the meeting be held at Ralph's house for two reasons. Ralph's wife has bridge club on tuesday nights and the dog next door to Weak-Eyes had eaten the last hind quarter it was going to get off of us. The buck wasn't that big to start with.

Meeting Adjourned.

Barney

P.S.

Ralph sings one heck of a mean baritone. We'll have to finish the season tomorrow night if the buck's thawed.

Closing Thought

When the hunt is over
    and your days in camp are through

The nicest thing your hunting friends
    could ever say or do

Is when they bring your name up
    They tell folks far and near

"That guy? Why he's a campmate,
    and man, can he hunt deer."

Mert

Printed in the U.S.A. by:
Rice Lake Printery, Inc.
627 South Main
Rice Lake, WI 54868